Your
City Garden

BOOKS BY JACK KRAMER IN THIS SERIES

Water Gardening
Miniature Plants Indoors and Out
Garden Planning for the Small Property
Hanging Gardens
Gardening with Stone and Sand
The Natural Way to Pest-Free Gardening
Ferns and Palms for Interior Decoration
(*Other titles in preparation*)

YOUR CITY GARDEN

Planning and Plants

By JACK KRAMER

Decorative drawings by Charles Hoeppner
How-to and plan drawings by Adrian Martinez

CHARLES SCRIBNER'S SONS · New York

A—1.73 [MZ]

Printed in the United States of America
Library of Congress Catalog Card Number: 72-1204
SBN 684-13029-7 (cloth)
SBN 684-13028-9 (paper, SL)

Contents

Introduction:
The Ultimate Retreat

Today our cities are more crowded than ever, with more than 70 percent of our population living in metropolitan areas. Increasing air and noise pollution make one want to run to the park or country or better yet to his own sylvan setting. Gardening in the city is no longer a luxury; it is becoming a necessity, and even the smallest backyard garden or tiny balcony is more important than it was years ago.

City gardens differ considerably from the normal suburban or rural garden. Space is the critical factor. Space is density to the developer and density is money in our society. So the city garden is generally confined to a small area, and ingenuity and careful planning are essential to get the most from the least. Usually, the city gardener does not have too much time to work in his garden, so plants that can tolerate adverse conditions and that once established can take care of themselves, must be selected. Elaborate gardens on the grand scale are out; the small retreat is desirable. Although it may be postage-stamp size, it can still be a charming garden and afford the city dweller a chance to work with nature and have nature work for him. Plants not only help to alleviate air pollution, they also act as noise barriers in crowded cities.

City gardens can be in the sky—on rooftops and balconies—or on the ground—in the backyard or courtyard. Each of these areas offers a challenge. There is simply no easy way to a lovely greenery without some work, however, for sky gardens are besieged with wind and hot sun, and on-the-ground gardens are generally shaded. Yet with intelligent planning and proper selection of plant materials, nature can be part of everyday living where it never existed before.

The garden in the city may not be as grand or glorious as in the country but a little bit of greenery in your immediate surroundings goes a long way to make each day more cheerful and special. The city garden can be a jewel tucked between brick and stone walls, and even the renter can achieve a feeling of a permanent garden. The city garden, you will find, is worth its space in gold.

Jack Kramer

1. Your Garden in the City ✍

Two things that hinder successful gardening—air pollution and excessive shade—are present in the city, and yet here is where you need the sylvan setting most, more so than in the country, where nature lends a helping hand. A fantastic garden in a city situation gives the heart joy and the soul solace, and there is keen satisfaction in working with the elements. Today's city garden can be a jewel, but because of increasing pollution it is important to know more about plants and their relationship to the environment if you want your garden to be successful. City gardening is certainly not impossible, but it takes planning, careful plant selection, and perseverance.

LOCATION

To start your garden, take inventory of what space you have. Because there probably won't be too many places where you can develop the garden, consider carefully the area available. Are there any vistas from the property that are outstanding and worth keeping? Or does concrete abound on all sides? (What is *around* the garden is as important as what goes *into* it.) Realize the disadvantages first, so you can cope intelligently with them later when you must.

What about the orientation of the garden? Pay attention to the sun and how it strikes the property; without sufficient light, good plant growth will be difficult (but not impossible). In most instances a southerly exposure is the warmest and most satisfying for outdoor living and for plants, but if this isn't available, a northern cool garden with lots of shade-tolerant plants can also be a fine retreat in the city. If the property is hilly consider interesting levels or terraces;

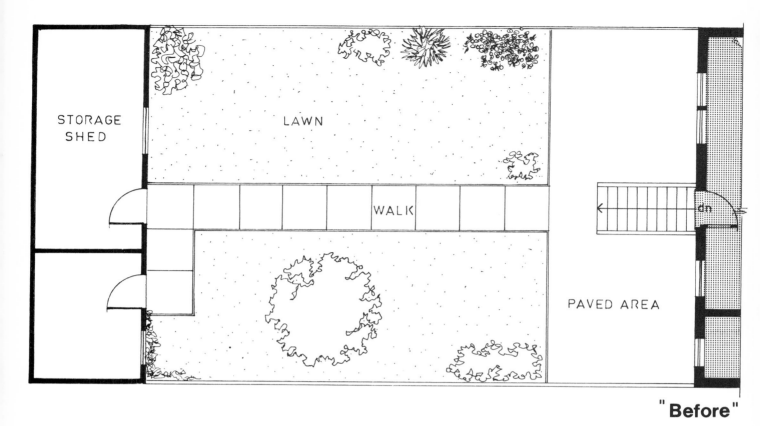

STORAGE
SHED

LAWN

WALK

PAVED AREA

dn

"Before"

LAWN

STORAGE UNDER DECK

dn

DECK

dn

DECK

PLANT ROOM

dn

POOL

"After"

Typical backyard. (Drawing by Adrian Martinez)

they add a variety to space that is constantly interesting to the eye. If there is a city skyline view (and this is *not* a disadvantage), frame it with trees and shrubs for a handsome picture. If there is no view at all (and this is often the case), develop dramatic interests within the boundaries of the garden. Use specimen plantings, standards, and espaliers to decorate and distract and to make a picture in itself. Sculpture, fountains, and gazebos are other ways of keeping the eye within the confines of the garden.

You'll find there are many places on your property (small though they may be) where a desirable garden can be created. First consider ground-level gardens—front, rear, and side. Which would be best for the garden? (Each area must be handled differently.) What about a lovely roof garden? If you are an apartment dweller, deck and balcony gardens are well within your means and can be handsome small greeneries.

This city garden faces north, and sun is blocked by the building next to it. Still, it is a handsome scene. Shade-tolerant plants like acanthus are used; other plant material is at a minimum, yet there is enough to provide beauty. (Photo by Matthew Barr)

A lovely reflecting pool and waterfall is part of this city garden carefully framed with large-leaved and small-leaved plants. A brick wall further enhances the garden corner. (Drawing by Charles Hoeppner)

GROUND-LEVEL GARDENS

Ground-level gardens are popular because they are part of the home and can make a small house appear larger, especially if you open the windows to "bring in" the outdoors. Use small flowering trees, handsome evergreens, and screening hedges. And don't forget easy-maintenance ground covers massed together to create a carpet of greenery. Concentrate on spring bulbs planted for early, seasonal color and superb in any situation. Incorporate a small paved area to provide a place for chairs and tables. A paved floor with even a few container plants will be a low-maintenance garden, yet handsome.

The front garden borders the street and provides direct access to the residence. Here privacy is a critical factor, and often, as with typical brownstones, the garden area will either be below the sidewalk level in an areaway or 2 to 3 feet above it. When the garden area is above the sidewalk, a retaining wall usually forms the basis for the private upper garden. If the garden is sunken, it can be a quiet greenery entrance to the lower unit. A tree for some shade and some potted plants (with fencing for security) brings a most attractive touch of green to this lower unit.

With more space than average, a south rear city garden makes a lovely picture. Flowering plants, evergreens, and lacy-leaved trees make this a pleasant spot. (Photo by Ken Molino)

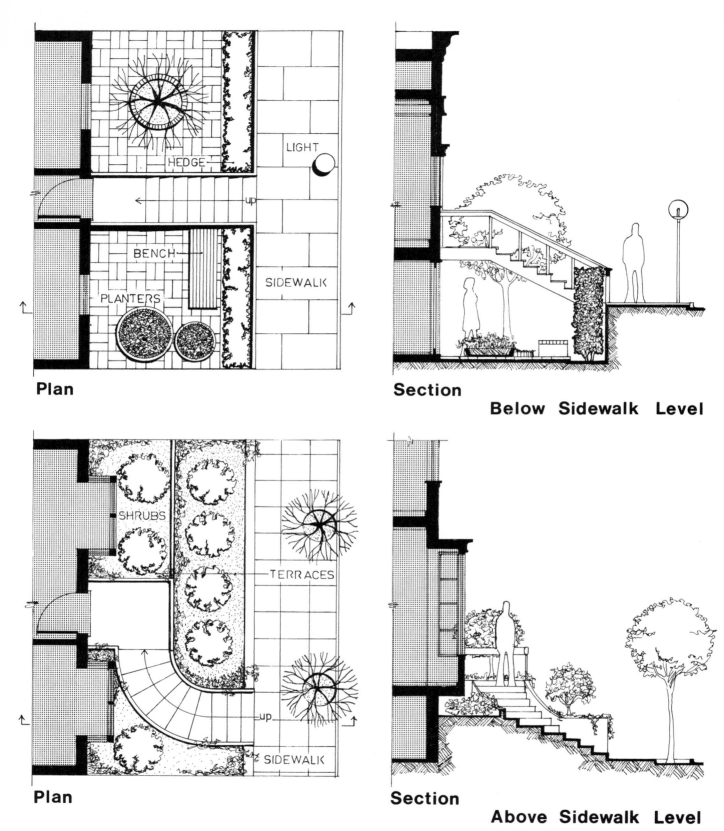

Plan

HEDGE

LIGHT

up

BENCH

SIDEWALK

PLANTERS

Section

Below Sidewalk Level

Plan

SHRUBS

TERRACES

up

SIDEWALK

Section

Above Sidewalk Level

City front yard. (Drawing by Adrian Martinez)

The rear or backyard area is usually the most popular space for the typical urban garden. Here is where you can use your ingenuity to create a closed-yet-open landscape, even in the smallest area.

If the rear property has parking or outbuildings, consider a side-yard garden. These narrow areas are more desirable for plants than you may think, and don't forget that this garden spot can be viewed from the windows of your rooms. Side gardens can be dramatic with proper plant selection: strive for an intimate, but cozy scene.

Doorway gardens should not be neglected; this shows a handsome treatment of brick and plants . . . a charming entrance. (Drawing by Charles Hoeppner)

For a postage-stamp-size city garden this setting has been well managed; one large shrub, ground cover, and a brick wall for old world charm. (Drawing by Charles Hoeppner)

HOUSE INTERIOR

FENCE

POTTED PLANTS

BUILT-IN SEAT

FLOWERS

POOL

STONE PAVED PATIO

TERRACED PLANTERS

TREE

SHRUBS

GATE

POTTING & STORAGE SHED

Plan: 25' x 40' lot

Narrow backyard. (Drawing by Adrian Martinez)

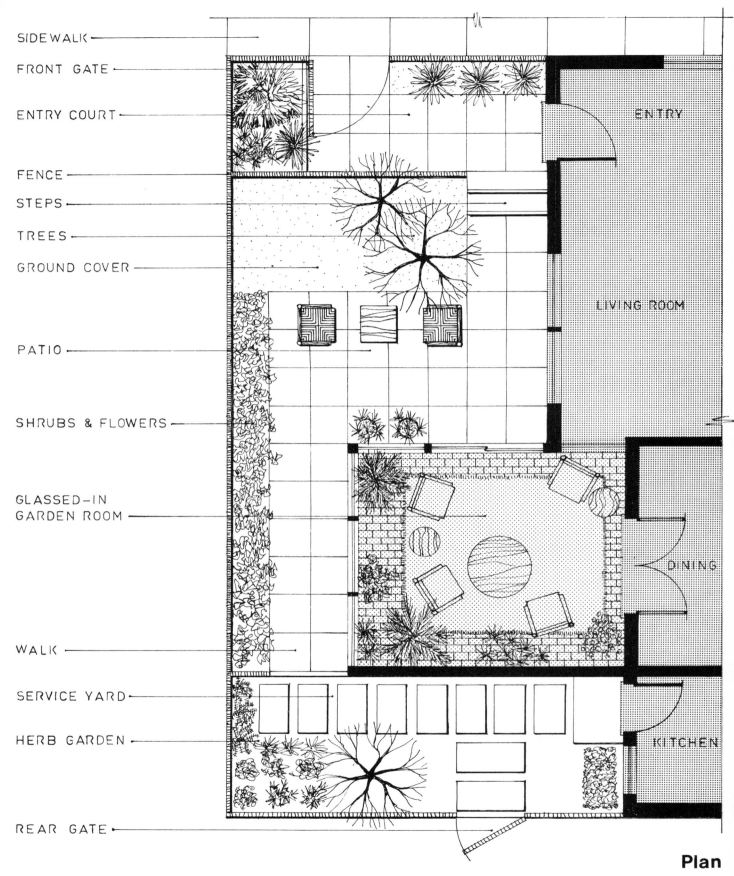

SIDEWALK

FRONT GATE

ENTRY COURT

FENCE

STEPS

TREES

GROUND COVER

PATIO

SHRUBS & FLOWERS

GLASSED-IN
GARDEN ROOM

WALK

SERVICE YARD

HERB GARDEN

REAR GATE

ENTRY

LIVING ROOM

DINING

KITCHEN

Plan

Side yard. (Drawing by Adrian Martinez)

Facing the street, this city garden is the welcoming scene for guests to the house. Privacy is afforded by screens and fences. Evergreens and ground covers pre-dominate. (Photo by Matthew Barr)

This side yard garden is a study in textures and contrasts, and yet it all works well together. Its main premise is plants in pots. (Photo by Matthew Barr)

GARDENS IN THE SKY

Balcony and roof gardens are always a challenge. The former is generally an awkward, small area, and the garden on top of a building is subject to wind and scorching sun. Yet a bright green scene in each area is possible. Each place deserves and needs special treatment, but both try to create a pleasant foreground for the distant urban view. Use tall plants in tubs on the sides to screen you from neighbors and to create a feeling of enclosure; use smaller plants and flowers in pots to give the excitement of color. However, do not fence yourself in.

A small balcony need not be bare; here container plants give it dimension and beauty and . . . little maintenance. (Photo by Matthew Barr)

A roof garden that is indeed a prize in the city, this handsome greenery is resplendent in roses and other flowering plants. (Photo by Matthew Barr)

Roof gardens are elegant and can be stunning. Don't let surroundings like wires or poles bother you; with careful planning they can be camouflaged. Generally, there is more space to work with here than in ground gardens, and the garden on top of the world is unique. Sun and wind, although potential problems, can easily be coped with by using shade screens, canopies, and so forth. You need to know something about building construction for this garden. What is the roofing material? Will the structure support a garden? How will the drainage be handled? Is the roof of a good quality so that leaks and repairs will not be a problem? How do you get to the garden from the floor below?

In the following chapters we shall consider all these types of gardens and how to plan and plant them for maximum pleasure.

2. Designing the Garden ✍

There are two schools of thought on designing a city garden. Some gardeners suggest random plantings, using fill-in material later. Others, and I am one, strongly urge you to plan the garden before you start. This is especially true in places where every inch of space counts. Why not create a total harmonious scene rather than a hodge-podge of plants?

Although design and planning do take time in the beginning, they save money and work later. It is far better to plant *what will grow* in your garden rather than experiment with plants that may need replacing later. A terrace, patio, or small pool is another consideration; space has to be reserved at the start for these garden features, not later when things are in place.

Containers and planters, flower beds, and vegetable gardens are other advantages of even the smallest garden. You can have vegetables in tubs if there isn't extensive ground—tomatoes, cucumbers, and squash are all possibilities. And even diminutive flower beds will yield some flowers for indoors.

Types of Gardens
Through the centuries man has always tried to beautify his surroundings by gardening. There were the famous Hanging Gardens of Babylon (built around 600 B.C.). The ancient Persians and Egyptians built houses around open courtyards, and the Greeks blended grand architecture with detailed landscaping—flower beds, pools, stately trees, and pot plants. Symmetry was the theme in Greek gardens. The Romans were skillful gardeners, too, and the garden pavilions of

16

Rome are still known today. However, gardening and landscaping truly blossomed during the eighteenth century in the Italian and French villas and palaces and in the country manors of England. These were huge, symmetrical and beautiful formal gardens, but they were impractical. Later, the British restyled gardening and produced the more natural garden, ending formality. Houses and grounds were smaller, and a new type of garden was initiated.

In colonial America the garden was only a place to grow flowers. Now, of course, it is a way of life—the extra living space. Today, the average city property is even smaller than it was ten years ago, and the cost of land has reduced the garden to a small area.

Today's garden demands something different from what has been done in the past. New structural and synthetic materials, new plants, and new ways of growing things make today's gardening an exciting adventure.

Formal and informal gardens have been popular for years, but the average city lot is too small to accommodate either one. The formal

Part terrace, part garden, this city site emphasizes the formal type garden; a lovely place to relax and enjoy nature, and maintenance is minimum. (Photo by Max Eckert. Designer: John Astin Perkins, AIA, AID, Dallas, Texas)

plan needs vast areas, which is impossible with city property. It is like a mirror; one side reflects the other, creating symmetry. The resulting geometric pattern can be pleasing when it suits the house, but generally you need much land.

The informal or natural landscape also has drawbacks. You must have old trees and shrubs, but often they aren't on city plots. Neglected city gardens are generally in poor shape, and a keen eye is necessary to observe and save any remnants of trees or shrubs. Occas-

A formal and lovely backyard garden that, although small, provides the necessary green to this city site. Hedges are the mainstay of the garden. (Drawing by Charles Hoeppner)

This backyard garden depends on the beauty of brick laced with vines. Ground cover lines the base of the wall and one tree is a necessary decorative accent. (Drawing by Charles Hoeppner)

ionally, careful pruning and cutting can transform plant materials into useful trees or shrubs. Restoring them to health takes a little more time.

The informal or natural theme depends on asymmetrical balance, that is, no pairs of trees or shrubs, no straight lines or borders. It is a continuous flow of plant material and, as such, is ideally suited to confined areas.

Most of today's garden plans depend on both formal and informal qualities. Climate will also affect what type of landscape to select, and the nature of the site is equally important.

Scale, Proportion, and Unity

Plants have definite forms. They are spreading or horizontal, round or globular, weeping or trailing, and vertical (pyramidal) or columnar in shape. Dogwood, pin oak, and hawthorn have strong horizontal

A corner niche becomes a garden in a city lot and the feeling is predominantly formal; the cascading fountain and small pool capture the eye immediately. (Photo by Molly Adams)

Bricks present a formal picture in this garden further enhanced by a pair of lovely stone containers. (Photo by Molly Adams. Designer: Alice Ireys, LA)

lines and carry the eye from one plant to another. For low flat houses, these are good selections. Beech, flowering cherry, and weeping willow are delicate and fragile in appearance and create softer lines. They are good in front of stiffer-looking subjects.

The form of a plant is vitally important in landscaping. Unless you know what the plant will look like when it is mature, selecting form is somewhat like a guessing game. When you make selections, try to visualize the plant fully grown. Some species lose their symmetrical form with age. Others, like pines and some firs, lose their lower branches as they get older. Scale and proportion must be carefully considered in landscaping because they are, perhaps, the keys to an attractive setting.

Scale is the visual relationship of each form to every other form and to the design as a whole. It can be called a relationship of size. You must establish an appealing scale relationship between the garden and the house. The starting point can be a tree. A large tree will link the house and the garden together; it will be part of the joining process. With a small house, plant a small tree. However, the principle can be altered. Use a very large tree with a small house and you will make the house seem charming. Creating an illusion of space with plant materials is an exciting kind of landscaping.

A charming lightpost is the focus of this small city garden. The single tree is sculptural. Scale, proportion, and unity of materials are well planned here. (Drawing by Charles Hoeppner)

Proportion is the harmonious relationship of one part of a total picture to another and to the whole. A large paved terrace and a small lawn can be in proportion; on another site the patio can be small and the lawn large. To make both areas the same size is a mistake because then there is no interest, one element does not complement the other. Balance vertical forms with several horizontal elements.

22

Unity in a composition is the putting together of materials so that they become whole. You do not want a hodgepodge of unrelated masses insulting the eye. Plants of related forms, colors, and textures, well chosen, achieve the unity every attractive garden needs.

Another element to consider is rhythm in the composition. This involves repeating the same group of plants to give a sense of movement and balance—having elements of similar size, form, and emphasis for use as one feature.

If you study each term individually, you will see that one depends on the other and that they are all interrelated. Generally, if you get the scale and proportion right, the other elements fall into line.

Planning on Paper

Planning on paper saves much unnecessary labor later. You don't have to draw a general ground plan to scale for the property; you can merely make a sketch. Using your plan as a guide, mark the location of the house and its boundary lines onto graph paper, letting each square equal 1 foot. Draw the outline of the house and include steps, walks, driveways, trees, and shrubs.

This Japanese styled garden may be small but it is superbly landscaped. Note the clever intermingling of textures and tones. (Photo by Matthew Barr)

A natural garden is presented in a city backyard with abundant plant material accented with a pair of sculptural trees. (Photo by Matthew Barr)

You must also determine the ground slope. Stretch a string cross-ways across the plot. Use a mason's level on the string and measure the distance between the ground and the string to determine how much of a grade there is. Record the high and low areas and how much the grade drops on the graph paper. Put in sun, shade, and north-point designations. Study the composition; if all the present features are on the graph paper, start planning the garden.

24

Now, lay a sheet of tracing paper over the graph paper. Sketch traffic patterns first on the tracing paper. Draw rough sizes and shapes desired for outdoor objects: terrace, garden beds, planters, new trees and shrubs, play and service areas, etc. The shapes drawn should start to relate to each other. (Start again with a new piece of tracing paper if you're not satisfied.) Consider all things carefully and make several plans so that all the family can agree. Remember that many plants in city gardens are in containers—boxes and tubs. Study carefully the types of containers possible (do-it-yourself containers and commercial ones) so you will know what to use (see Chapter 7).

Once you have a satisfactory sketch, make a detailed design. Be sure to have the exact measurements of the house and lot, outdoor objects, and existing plant material. Decide how much construction will be necessary in the garden—fences, terraces, pools, walls—and how much planting will be needed.

The following patterns will help you plan:

Rectangular or square patterns. These are the easiest and most natural. They are usually projections of the house form. Working with a uniform module (a space repeated again and again) simplifies a plan. The module can be 3 x 4 feet or 5 x 5 feet, or any other suitable size. You can pave the patio with 3- x 4-foot blocks, use stepping stones of the same size, and plant islands and beds that will relate to the same module. Thus, every design line is in proportion and visually pleasing. Your pattern will be simple but concisely organized.

Acute or obtuse angles or triangles. These reflect the angular form of the house and site, provide a focal point for the eye, and provide a sense of space and direction.

Circular forms. Circular forms add interest to the pattern. When properly balanced with straight lines, they present an attractive picture.

Free curves. These curving lines have an ever-changing radius. These sweeping natural lines produce richness in motion when skillfully used with geometric forms.

From these basic patterns any number of combinations of forms can be drawn.

3. Backyard Gardens 🖋

With today's effort to beautify America, backyard gardens are becoming vitally important in our scheme of living. The garden is no longer left to develop haphazardly; more often it is turned into a necessary greenery amid concrete buildings. And in all cities from San Francisco to Chicago to New York, the house with even a small garden has a better chance of selling than the house without greenery.

Since nature around us is fast dwindling, we naturally desire to bring it back to us through plants in city conditions, both indoors and out. All kinds of small, intimate, and charming gardens are appearing in our cities, replacing former eyesores. Our plant-a-tree program has carried over to the average homeowner, and city gardens are becoming a challenge that offers satisfaction, beauty, and, most importantly, a place to retreat to when necessary.

This new interest has brought about changing ideas in design and new plants—plants that can cope with polluted air and formerly untenable city situations.

CHARACTERISTICS

No matter how small your property, with design and planning you can create a garden. Although the limitations of the site can influence the garden, ingenuity will play a great part in making it pleasant. The only restriction in designing the small backyard garden is amount—don't put too much in too small an area. Concentrate on a simple but attractive plan that will serve the functions of the family and offer an attractive picture.

The informal character of this garden perfectly suits the architecture of the house; it all blends into a pleasing picture in the city. (Photo by Matthew Barr)

Of course, the garden should suit the house and be in character with its architecture, but this is more easily said than done. It may take several years to really coordinate plants, land and house. But if you start right you can add to the plan as years go by.

Remember the limitations of backyard gardens. Generally the area is small, and *very informal* gardens that imitate nature are difficult to create. Usually a cohesive but simple design will create the most happy expression of plants and land. The full effects of the garden must be created completely within the narrow boundaries of the backyard site. To achieve a measure of success the garden should be an extension of the house like an outdoor room. The fundamentals of good design as outlined in Chapter 2 apply to the backyard garden, but rigid plans are impossible because each site and each climate is different. What you ultimately choose depends on you, your family, and your specific site.

Fences, Screens, Pavings

Fences and screens, walks and pavings are all part of the backyard garden. If possible, also include a small terrace, which is the stepping stone to, or link between, the house and garden. In city situations, fences are really an integral part of the garden, always visible. Use decorative, high-styled designs made of concrete blocks,

This is a small house, almost a cottage, and the garden is in good proportion to the house, neither too large nor too small, and yet affords a handsome greenery. (Photo by Matthew Barr)

A unique fence is part of the decor of this home; it adds eye interest and a backdrop for bamboo in planters. (Photo by Ken Molino)

brick, or wood. Wood is informal in character and always handsome; brick is somewhat formal, but it has great charm; and concrete blocks available in many designs are dramatic although somewhat sterile. There are many new materials for fencing, so investigate and study them before you make a final choice. Some fences will be suitable for do-it-yourself projects, while others will require professional help.

Many people prefer the ultimate in privacy, in which case complete walls are necessary. However, a more pleasant arrangement is a fretwork or gridtype fence that allows air to enter but still obscures vision enough to ensure partial privacy.

The choice of patio pavings is almost limitless, from brick to tile to slate to concrete and so on. What you use depends on how large the area is and how much pattern you want in your garden. Like carpets in the home, pavings should be used to make a small area larger, a large area smaller. And, no matter which paving you use, repeat the material somewhere to provide the desired unity.

OVERHEADS AND CANOPIES

I mention overheads and canopies for the small garden because they provide privacy, add decoration, and make the area an all-weather place. Overheads can be partial coverings—lath, canvas strips—or solid ceilings of fiberglass. Decide how much sun the plants need, how much shade for comfort you want, and how decorative you want the overhead to be (to soften the harsh lines of concrete walls). Trellises or arbors decorated with vines will be an ever-pleasing canopy of green. Brightly colored canvas enlivens the city garden: the design can be simple or elegant with canvas or wood structures.

One popular overhead is an open framework of wood. It is actually a wood grid with cross members 2 to 6 inches apart. Another good ceiling is lattice and lath or plain lath. Use 2- x 2-inch lumber spaced 2

A small wood awning on this garden affords some privacy and protection from rain. (Photo by Matthew Barr)

Espaliers do a great deal to cover bare walls and add accent in a city garden; holly is used here. (Photo by Matthew Barr)

inches apart supported by 2- x 10-inch beams. Support the roof with 2- x 6-inch posts spaced about 2 feet apart and set in concrete piers. Louvered boards are another overhead idea, and ¼-inch exterior plywood can be used, too.

Plastic paneling is popular because it can be easily sawed or drilled and comes in several colors. It is available flat or corrugated but does have a disadvantage: it rattles in the wind. Woven canvas strips in a basket-weave design give ventilation and yet offer some protection from direct sun. Set the wood frame in place first; use 4- x 4-inch posts in preset concrete piers. Be sure the frame is rigid and does not wobble. Lace canvas over and under the beam supports.

Corregated metal awnings are occasionally used for overhangs, but they are rarely attractive. If cost is important, consider bamboo blinds that roll up and down like a window curtain. On a metal or wooden frame they can be easily controlled with draw cords.

More sophisticated roofing designs include movable glass or plastic ceilings. These designs incorporate motorized drive units and electric-cord take-up reels. The movable roof slides open to admit sun and closed to keep out wind or rain. These units are certainly convenient, but they are also expensive.

31

PLANT MATERIAL

TREES

Trees are the mainstay of any garden, including the small city site. Generally, one large tree is about all backyards can accommodate, but two or three smaller trees should be used also to balance the scene and provide scale.

Flowering trees are generally small by nature, and some are ideal for backyard sites. Compact and colorful, they add great beauty, and with minimum care they grow well even in adverse conditions. The flowering dogwood (*Cornus florida*) is always a good choice, as is the English hawthorn (*Crataegus*), with white flowers and red berries. The fringe tree (*Chionanthus*) seldom grows more than 25 feet high and is a bower of white flowers in spring. The sourwood (*Oxydendrum arboreum*) and some of the locusts (*Robinia*) are other fine choices. And don't forget magnolias. Some of the small ones like M. *soulangiana* offer a wealth of color.

The fast-growing trees like birch, willow, and poplar are fine city-garden candidates because they grow in almost any soil and tolerate neglect. Catalpa is another no-nonsense tree, and, of course, ailanthus is always satisfactory, if not well liked.

Needled evergreen trees (conifers) are necessary for winter color and dimension in a garden; they make a bold statement. However, evergreens need good air circulation to thrive, a commodity that is sometimes severely lacking in city conditions. For this reason it is sometimes more prudent to select the broad-leafed evergreens (those with wide leaves) for the city site, since many can tolerate somewhat adverse conditions if necessary.

Because conifers are green all winter, you should include a few in your garden. For best results varieties of yew (*Taxus*) are the choicest selections. Unlike some evergreens, yews retain their dark green color all winter long, lend themselves to pruning, and come in two shapes: upright and flat top.

Arborvitae (*Thuja*), a popular tree, is, unfortunately, difficult to grow; some species turn brown in winter or lose bottom branches. Rather than arborvitae, and if you don't favor yews, try dark needled hemlocks (*Tsuga*); these are fine graceful trees that grow quickly and can tolerate a shady situation. Furthermore, they come in pyramidal, globe or columnar varieties.

Pfitzer juniper (*Juniperus pfitzeriana*) has been recommended by experts for many years, and rightly so. It is robust, has lovely blue-green foliage, and succeeds well in city situations. But it will need a little sun. The deodar cedar (*Cedrus deodara*) and the Norway spruce (*Picea abies*) are other candidates for city sites.

Any garden with broad-leaf evergreens is an attractive greenery; even a few plants add greatly to an area. Many broad-leaf varieties tolerate shade with impunity, prefer acidity (which is generally found in city soils), withstand soot and smoke to a remarkable degree, have a compact habit of growth, and need little pruning.

Rhododendrons (including azalea) are the most useful group of broad-leaf plants. There are hundreds available. Rhododendrons are spectacular in bloom and yet are still attractive without flowers.

Ground covers dramatize a situation and appear handsome with concrete in this unique treatment. (Photo by Ken Molino)

Vines are the workhorse of the city garden to provide privacy and beauty, and even if they do become sort of a jungle, they are still pleasing to see. (Photo by Matthew Barr)

Azaleas too are stellar plants that offer a wealth of color and beauty. Because there are so many, it is impossible to list specific varieties; but your nursery will have quite a choice of flowers, colors, and forms. Most will succeed in city gardens; rhododendrons will even bloom in shade, although azaleas need a little sun. All, however, must be copiously watered in summer, for they suffer more than most plants if soil dries out. Several new varieties of the beautiful *Camellia japonica* will survive even zero temperatures and perform well in shade, and you can depend on them to bloom yearly.

The Japanese holly (*Ilex crenata*), although not as showy as rhododendrons or camellias, is a reliable performer that tolerates shade and soot and still has fine green color. There are many good varieties and some bad ones, so choose carefully. English holly (*I. aquifolium*) and American holly (*I. opaca*) are good choices. The former has dark green leaves and the latter has pale green foliage. Both require some sun to prosper. If you want the decorative berries, you must plant both the male and female species.

Japanese andromeda (*Pieris japonica*) is a good choice because it has some clusters of white flowers and does very well in untoward conditions. *Euonymus* species, *Mahonia aquifolium*, barberry (*Berberis*), *Acuba*, *Pyracantha*, and some cotoneasters are rewarding too.

For other trees and shrubs see the list at the end of this chapter.

Ground covers, container plants, and vines are used in this city backyard with brick paving. The effect is totally charming. Note the wooden planters throughout to give dimension to the garden. (Photo by Matthew Barr)

GROUND COVERS AND VINES

Ground covers and vines should not be ignored by city gardeners. Vines cover a multitude of sins—unsightly walls, awkward corners—and flowering vines are majestic in bloom. Ground covers are low-maintenance, rewarding plants that take the work out of gardening. Lawns need much attention and will keep you forever busy, but ground covers practically grow by themselves once established, and there are so many lovely ones to choose from.

If this section seems heavy with plant suggestions, it is because prudent selection of ground covers and vines can make a city garden sing with color. And generally, although you can only accommodate a few trees and perhaps three or four shrubs in your garden, ground covers and vines find ready places. Evergreen ground covers are attractive in summer and winter. Many grow in shade, and others tolerate full sun and even drought. These are tough plants, sure to please. Most nurseries will tell you to place ground covers 12 to 16 inches apart, but that way it will take almost two, maybe three, years for full coverage of an area. Instead, place them closer together and have a lush green carpet in a short time.

VINES

BOTANICAL AND COMMON NAME	DESCRIPTION
Akebia quinata (five-leaf akebia)	Vigorous twiner; fragrant small flowers. Sun or partial shade.
Ampelopsis brevipedunculata (blueberry climber)	Strong grower with dense leaves. Sun or shade.
Aristolochia durior (Dutchman's pipe)	Big twiner with mammoth leaves. Sun or shade.
Clematis armandi (evergreen clematis)	Lovely flowers and foliage. Sun.
Euonymus fortunei (winter creeper)	Shiny, leathery leaves; orange berries in fall. Sun or shade.
Hedera helix (English ivy)	Scalloped neat leaves; many varieties. Shade.
Hydrangea petiolaris (climbing hydrangea)	Heads of snowy flowers. Sun or partial shade.
Ipomoea purpurea (morning glory)	Flowers are white, blue, purple, pink, or red. Sun.

Lonicera japonica halliana (Hall's honeysuckle)	Deep green leaves, bronze in fall. Sun or shade.
Parthenocissus quinquefolia (Virginia creeper)	Scarlet leaves in fall. Sun or shade.
Pueraria thunbergiana (kudsuo vine)	Purple flowers. Sun or partial shade.
Rosa (rambler rose)	Many varieties. Sun.
Vitis coignetiae (glory grape)	Colorful autumn leaves. Sun or partial shade.
Wisteria floribunda (Japanese wisteria)	Violet-blue flowers. Sun.

Note: unless otherwise stated, all vines hardy to approximately −15°F.

GROUND COVERS

BOTANICAL AND COMMON NAME	DESCRIPTION
Ajuga	Rosettes of dark green leaves and spikes of blue flowers. Sun or shade.
Anthemis nobilis (camomile)	Light green, fernlike leaves. Sun.
Asarum caudatum	Attractive, heart-shaped leaves. Shade.
Cotoneaster (many species)	Shrubby, with small leaves and decorative berries. Sun.
Cryophytum crystallinum (ice plant)	Stiff leaves and bright daisylike flowers. Sun.
Epimedium	Semi-evergreen, with glossy leaves and dainty flowers. Partial shade.
Hosta (plantain lily)	Some with large leaves, others with small leaves. Shade.
Iberis sempervirens (evergreen candytuft)	Dense little bushes with white flowers. Sun.
Juniperus (see shrubs)	
Lonicera japonica halliana (Hall's honeysuckle)	Tough rampant vine. Sun or shade.
Pachysandra terminalis (Japanese pachysandra)	Whorls of dark green leaves. Shade.
Rosmarinus officinalis prostratus (rosemary)	Narrow leaves and blue flowers in spring. Sun.

SHRUBS

BOTANICAL AND COMMON NAME	DESCRIPTION
Aesculus parviflora (bottlebrush buckeye)	White flowers in July; grows 8 to 12 feet. Hardy to —10° F.
Aralia elata (Japanese angelica tree)	Small black berries. Grows to 45 feet. Hardy to —35° F.
Azalea (rhododendron)	Hundreds of varieties in many different groups. Most evergreen or semi-evergreen; others deciduous. Spectacular color. Needs acid soil.
Berberis thunbergi (Japanese barberry)	Graceful with arching stems. Deep green foliage and fiery red berries in fall. Deciduous. Hardy to —5° F.
Buddleia davidi (butterfly bush)	Dark green tapering leaves; small fragrant flowers in midsummer. Deciduous or semi-evergreen shrub. Hardy to —10° F.
Chaenomeles japonica (Japanese quince)	Red flowers in early May. Deciduous. Hardy to —20° F.
Clematis paniculata (Japanese clematis)	Glossy dark green leaves; fragrant, creamy white flowers in late summer and fall.
Cornus paniculata (gray dogwood)	Upright in form; many branches. Hardy to —20° F.
C. sanguinea (bloodtwig dogwood)	Dark green leaves; blood-red foliage in fall. Hardy to —20° F.
C. stolonifera (red-osier dogwood)	Red fall color; creamy white flowers throughout summer into fall. Hardy to —20° F.
Cotoneaster horizontalis (rock spray)	Small, glossy, bright green leaves; white flowers; red fruit. Deciduous. Hardy to —10° F.
Deutzia scabra candidissima (snowflake deutzia)	Double white flowers; dull green leaves. Hardy to —10° F.
Elaeagnus angustifolia (Russian olive)	Deciduous tree to 20 feet. Silvery gray leaves; fragrant and small greenish-yellow flowers in early summer. Hardy to —35° F.
Euonymus (many varieties)	Good evergreen; grows to 20 feet. Hardy to —20° F.
Fatsia japonica (Japanese aralia)	Dark green, fanlike leaves. Evergreen shrub. Hardy to 10° F.
Hydrangea quercifolia (oakleaf hydrangea)	Creamy white flowers in June. Bronze or crimson leaves in fall. Decidous shrub. Hardy to —5° F.
Ilex glabra (inkberry)	Black berries. Evergreen. Grows to 9 feet. Hardy to —35° F.

Juniperus chinensis pfitzeriana (Pfitzer juniper)	Arching growth habit; sharp-needled, grey-green foliage. Evergreen. Hardy to —20° F.
Kerria japonica (kerria)	Rounded, graceful shrub; bright green leaves turn yellow in fall. Yellow flowers March to May. Deciduous. Hardy to —20° F.
Lagerstroemia indica (crape myrtle)	Bright flowers from July to September; mature leaves deep glossy green. Hardy to 10° F.
Lonicera (honeysuckle)	Vigorous shrubs or vines. Hardy to —10° F.
Mahonia aquifolium (Oregon grape holly)	Yellow flowers; edible blue-black berries. Hardy to —10° F.
Malus sargenti (Sargent crabapple)	Dense, broad shrub; dark green foliage. Fragrant white flowers; tiny red fruit. Hardy to —5° F.
Philadelphus coronarius (sweet mock orange)	Robust to 10 feet. Oval leaves and fragrant white flowers. Deciduous. Hardy to —20° F.
Pieris japonica (Japanese andromeda)	Dark green glossy leaves; snowy white flowers in drooping clusters. Hardy to —10° F.
Potentilla fruticosa (cinquefoil)	Yellow flowers in May; many varieties. Hardy to —35° F.
Prunus subhirtella (rosebud cherry)	A small tree. Hardy to 0° F.
Rhododendron	Hundreds of varieties—one prettier than the other. Check with local nursery for those suited to your climate. Needs acid soil.
Rosa multiflora (Japanese rose)	Flowers usually white. Floriferous and vigorous. Deciduous. Hardy to —10° F; grows to 10 feet.
R. rugosa (rugosa rose)	Glossy green leaves. Single or double flowers in a wide range of colors. Deciduous. Hardy to —35° F.
Spiraea thunbergii (thunberg spiraea)	Leathery branchlets and single white flowers. Deciduous. Hardy to —20° F.
Syringa vulgaris (common lilac)	Bulky shrub to 20 feet. Fragrant lilac flowers. Deciduous. Hardy to —35° F.
Viburnum dentatum (arrowwood)	Creamy white flowers and red autumn color. Evergreen. Hardy to —10° F; grows to 20 feet.
V. lantana (wayfaring tree)	Oval leaves turn red in fall; tiny white flowers. Deciduous. Hardy to —35° F.
Weigela (many varieties)	Vigorous growers; brilliant flowers. Some start blooming in May with flowers until June. Hardy to —10° F.
Wisteria sinensis (Chinese wisteria)	Violet-blue flower clusters. Slightly fragrant. Hardy to —5° F.

TREES

BOTANICAL AND COMMON NAME	DESCRIPTION
Abies concolor (white fir)	Narrow, pyramid-shaped to 120 feet; rapid grower. Bluish-green needles. Hardy to —20° F.
Acer platanoides (Norway maple)	Wide-crowned to 60 feet. Yellow leaves in fall; greenish-yellow flowers in spring. Deciduous. Hardy to —35° F.
Ailanthus altissima (tree of heaven)	Rapid grower to 50 feet. Greenish flowers followed by clusters of red-brown, winged fruits in late summer and fall. Deciduous. Hardy to —20° F.
Catalpa speciosa (western catalpa)	Round-headed 40- to 70-foot tree. Leaves to 12 inches long. Hardy to —10° F.
Crataegus oxyacantha (English hawthorn)	Round-headed to 15 feet. Densely branching; hardy to —20° F.
C. phaenopyrum (Washington hawthorn)	Broadly columnar to 30 feet. Red fall color. Hardy to —20° F.
Elaeagnus angustifolia (Russian olive)	Deciduous tree to 20 feet. Shedding, dark brown bark; silvery gray leaves. Small, and fragrant greenish-yellow flowers in early summer. Hardy to —50° F.
Euonymus europaea (spindle tree)	Retains leaves late in fall. Hardy to —20° F.
Fraxinus americana (white ash)	Straight trunk, oval-shaped crown. Grows to 100 feet; dense foliage. Hardy to —35° F.
Ginkgo biloba (ginkgo)	Wide-spreading deciduous tree. Light green leaves in spring and summer; gold in fall. Can grow 70 to 80 feet. Hardy to —20° F.
Gleditsia triacanthos (honey locust)	Rapid grower; upright trunk with spreading branches. Can grow to 70 feet; deciduous. Hardy to —20° F.
Magnolia grandiflora (southern magnolia)	Usually dense pyramidal form. Pure white flowers; evergreen. Grows to 90 feet. Hardy to 5° F.
M. soulangiana (saucer magnolia)	White to pink or purplish-red flowers. Deciduous. Hybrid; hardy to —10° F.
Phellodendron amurense (Amur corktree)	Heavy horizontal branches; grows 35 to 40 feet. Deciduous. Hardy to —35° F.
Picea pungens (Colorado spruce)	Stiff horizontal branches; grows to 100 feet. Hardy to —50° F.
Platanus acerifolia (London plane tree)	Rapid grower, 40 to 80 feet. Wide-spreading branches. Hardy to —5° F.

Quercus borealis (red oak)	Rapid growth to 90 feet; broad-spreading branches; round-topped crown. Deciduous. Hardy to —35° F.
Tilia cordata (small-leaved linden)	Densely pyramidal. Dark green leaves, silvery underneath. Grows 50 to 90 feet. Hardy to —35° F.
Tsuga caroliniana (Carolina hemlock)	Compact, pyramid-shaped tree. Grows to 75 feet. Hardy to —10° F.

EVERGEEN TREES

BOTANICAL AND COMMON NAME	DESCRIPTION
Abies concolor (white fir)	Narrow, pyramid-shaped to 120 feet; rapid grower. Bluish-green needles. Hardy to —20° F.
Cedrus atlantica (atlas cedar)	Widely pyramidal tree to 120 feet. Silvery to light green needles in bunches. Hardy to —5° F.
Chamaecyparis obtusa (Hinoki false cypress)	Broad pyramid to 120 feet. Glossy and green scalelike leaves. Hardy to —20° F.
C. pisifera (Sawara false cypress)	Pyramidal to 150 feet, with horizontal branching habit. Open foliage. Hardy to —35° F.
Cryptomeria japonica lobbi	Pyramid-shaped tree. Hardy to —5° F.
Juniperus virginiana (eastern red cedar)	Dense pyramid to 90 feet. Foliage varies, but usually scalelike. Hardy to —50° F.
Picea abies or excelsa (Norway spruce)	Pyramidal growth to 150 feet. Dark green needles. Hardy to —50° F.
Pinus bungeana (lacebark pine)	Rounded to pyramid shape, often with several trunks. Long, bright green needles. Grows to 75 feet. Hardy to —20° F.
P. densiflora (Japanese red pine)	Horizontal branching tree to 100 feet. Bright, bluish-green needles. Hardy to —20° F.
P. nigra (Austrian pine)	Dense, stout pyramid to 90 feet. Very dark green needles. Hardy to —20° F.
P. parviflora (Japanese white pine)	Dense pyramid to 90 feet. Wide-spreading branches, with bluish-green to gray needles. Hardy to —10° F.
Taxus baccata (English yew)	Dense branching; grows to about 60 feet. Dark green needles. Hardy to —5° F.
T. cuspidata 'Capitata' (Japanese yew)	Grows to 50 feet. Dark green needles. Hardy to —20° F.
Thuja occidentalis (American arborvitae)	Columnar growth to 60 feet. Bright green to yellow-green needles. Hardy to —50° F.
Tsuga canadensis (hemlock)	Long, slender, horizontal branches. Dark green needles; grows to 90 feet. Hardy to —35° F.

4. Gardens in the Sky (Rooftop Gardens) 🌿

Rooftop gardening is one of the oldest forms of gardening; the Greeks were masters at it. Today, because of overcrowded city conditions, a new interest in rooftop gardening has emerged, and rightly so. This is a unique and pleasant way to add a garden to the home when outdoor space is at a premium. A small city roof garden properly planned is a retreat in the midst of brick and concrete. It need not be a penthouse roof; practically any roof can be used. In Chicago, my next-door neighbors had a lush greenery atop a garage, and the windows of their two-story home were a perfect vantage point for viewing the pretty scene.

Rooftop gardening is a challenge because you are dealing with a different set of rules than the ones for ground gardening. Different design attitudes are also necessary to achieve an attractive garden in the air. A great many things contribute to the success of a roof garden, and perhaps more careful thought is necessary in construction and selection of plant material than in planning ground gardens. The several kinds of roof gardens are: tiny balconies; gardens on roofs (house or garage); and penthouse gardens or terraces, which are spacious and costly.

Is It Structurally Sound?

Before you start plunging plants into a rooftop situation, consider the practical requirements. Can the roof support the weight of soil and plants? In northern climates, roofs are built to endure heavy snow loads. Still, in winter remember that soil-filled, rain-

42

Clever landscaping marks this city rooftop garden. Rather than blocking the far buildings, the plants frame the scene. Note the wind barriers. (Drawing by Charles Hoeppner)

and snow-soaked boxes are particularly heavy. Everything on the roof—soil, plants, etc.—is grown in planters or in built-in beds, boxes, pots, or containers of some sort. Check with an architect or someone familiar with roof structures before you start your garden. Usually, roofs can take the extra weight, but it is always prudent to be sure.

The roof must also be perfectly watertight, or excess water draining from plants will create a batch of problems. Generally, roofs are built to be watertight, but through the years small leaks or cracks may have developed, so a coat of asphalt may be in order. Drainage must also be considered; excess water must freely drain off the structure. There should be no accumulation of water on the roof, for this will eventually lead to ceiling problems below, which is hardly desirable. Drain tiles connected to outlets are the answer. Be sure also that all plant boxes are constructed so that soil, leaves, and twigs do not wash into roof gutters. If they do, clogging will result and cause damage to the building.

Rooftop gardens must meet another requirement: they have to have railings or other obstructions to prevent accidents. People's safety must be considered. In addition, railings or fencing act as windbreaks because roof gardens can be blustery places.

Fencing is no longer the problem it used to be because there is a selection of materials—glass, plastic, wood—to work with. Construction can be a do-it-yourself project, but remember to create a visually pleasing scene.

Consider the type of flooring necessary for the garden; you can use roof asphalt as it is, but it is rarely attractive. Brick and tile are extremely heavy, and the roof may not hold the weight, but pea gravel and other similar materials (for example, fir bark) are good substitutes. These materials can be easily put in place, can almost be molded into patterns with your hands, and are inexpensive. The disadvantage is that periodically they must be renewed, but they can be replaced by other materials at will.

Only when you have solved the basic problems (support, drainage, barriers) should you start to think of the design of the garden.

Planning the Rooftop Garden

It is possible but not prudent to dump a load of soil on a roof and start gardening; generally, you will have a hell of a mess. Soil must be contained in wooden planters, raised beds, or ornamental pots. Container gardening is vastly popular, and rightly so, since it offers many advantages and few disadvantages. Plants can be moved about easily, and in winter pot plants can do double duty as decoration indoors. But make no mistake, although container gardening is an answer, it is not a complete solution. The rooftop garden, like any other garden, must be planned. Have numerous handsome planter boxes at various levels for eye interest, establish patterns on the floor or against the fences to create visual motion, and select a theme to unite the landscape. Will the scheme be Japanese, with a few stones and plants? informal, with a freedom of plant material? or

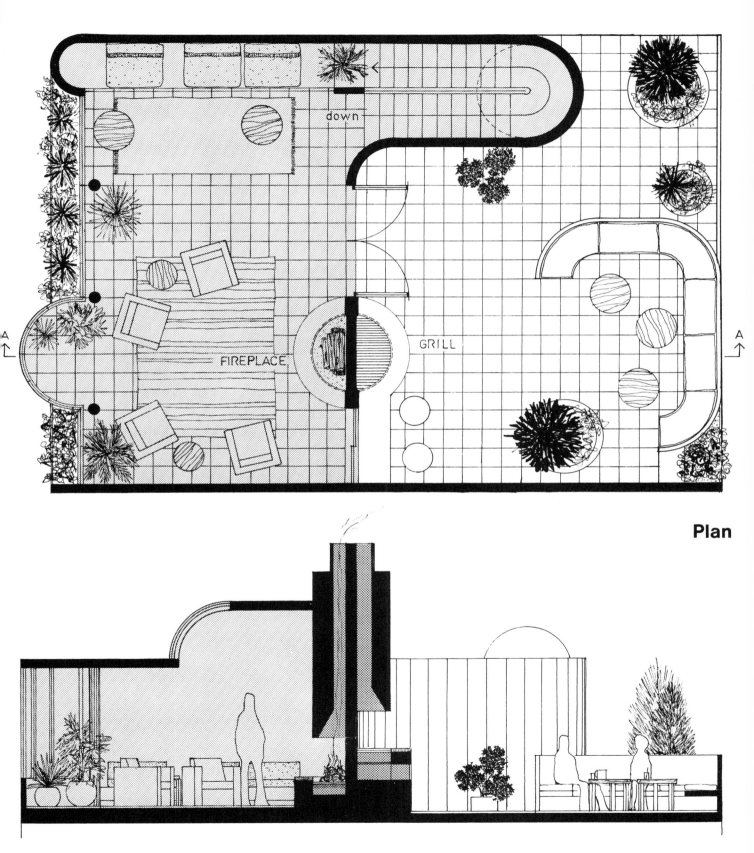

Plan

Section A-A

Roof garden. (Drawing by Adrian Martinez)

Inside the plan: down, FIREPLACE, GRILL

Tiered planters are effectively used in this roof garden. Note how the ivy has completely clothed the railings. (Photo by Matthew Barr)

somewhat formal, with few plants but simple and elegant lines? The garden in the air needs a great deal of planning to make it into an inviting retreat, but it can be done.

Use trellises and unusual fence designs to create beauty and a place for vines to grow. Consider a partial ceiling of some type to add a three-dimensional effect and to act as an overhead screen for privacy. A small awning or canopy can do worlds of good in a roof-top garden (see Chapter 3).

46

This is indeed a pleasing scene surrounded by greenery and an unmatched view of the bay and Marin County, California. (Photo by Matthew Barr)

WIND AND SUN PROTECTION

In the city, plants must contend with soot and air pollution. It has been proven that some plants can tolerate these alien conditions, but many cannot. Wind is another factor; it can quickly dessicate a plant (some varieties withstand wind with alacrity, but others are ruined by it). So a careful selection of plant material is almost essential if you want a thriving greenery that will not require too much time or money.

Wind increases evaporation in plants, which causes rapid dessication and injury to soft young leaves. Do install some wind protection so you won't constantly be replacing plants. Naturally, you should not enclose all sides with a fence or screen, for this would shut off views and create an overheated boxed-in space. Determine which is the windiest side and use buffers there. If you need more protection, consider louvered boards with spaces between them. A louvered fence lessens wind without blocking air circulation. Covered with climbing plants, these fences add a decorative note to the garden.

On a roof, direct sun can bake plants—people, too—so avoid this uncomfortable situation. Place arbors and trellises to distribute shade where it will be most needed.

PLANTING THE GARDEN

Many kinds of plants can be used in the rooftop garden, but you want an assemblage of interesting shrubs and trees of varied shapes and leaf patterns, accented with flowering beauties. Remember that in winter, unless you use evergreens, you must take the tender plants inside. Put them into an unheated but not-freezing garage or on a porch.

On a roof garden, plants have no help from surrounding greenery because around them there is either empty space or concrete and glass buildings. It is important to use bold and dramatic contrasting plants to create an intimate space.

Since a great deal of roof gardening is done in planters of different sizes and shapes, remember that wood boxes are easier to move than concrete or stone containers (see Chapter 7).

Trees and shrubs, annuals and perennials, almost any plant can be used for roof gardens, but, of course, some will do better than

All kinds of flowering plants edge this roof garden and provide a dramatic foil for the sparkling view. (Photo by Matthew Barr)

others (see list at end of chapter). And, since sun is one asset of sky-high gardens, don't forget vegetables and herbs. These plants grow beautifully, need no more care than flowers, and provide many rewards.

Rather than large trees, which are out of scale in roof gardens, use small trees with picturesque growth habits like weeping willow or crabapple. Multiple-stem trees are sculptural and break harsh lines; magnolia and gray birch are two outstanding types. These trees grow in an upright pattern and take little space.

Remember to use vines; they are excellent for covering an unsightly wall, making a tapestry of green on a trellis, or softening the edge of a planter. There are many wonderful flowering vines, and most adapt well to rooftop conditions (see Chapter 3 for choice vines).

Plantings in the rooftop garden have to withstand severe wind and sun in summer and cold in winter. Avoid tall-growing, weak-limbed trees. Even if you provide windbreaks, supplemental wire support may be necessary during extreme exposures. Wind can rock trees mercilessly and loosen roots. Use guy wires anchored in deep containers and be sure the portion that goes around the tree is sheathed in a piece of rubber.

Use mulches—peat moss, fir bark—over earth in containers to prevent rapid drying out and to help keep roots cool and moist. Prune trees and shrubs with care because there is usually more garden winterkill in the air than on the ground. In early spring, remove all dead wood—small twigs as well as large branches. Limbs rubbing against each other produce wounds in the bark through which diseases may enter. Trim away all wood broken by high winds.

Once again I want to mention moisture for the roof garden. Soil dries out more rapidly than it does on the ground garden, so slow, deep watering is necessary. Do not skimp on the water if you want lush plants.

Use planting boxes for vegetables; these cost little to make or buy. Soil is the big expense, but well worth it for your own produce. Buy the best soil you can get. You can save money if you know the planting depths of the vegetables you plan to grow. For instance, radishes and lettuce need only 3 to 4 inches of soil; carrots need deep beds. Spinach, tomatoes, and beets are other possibilities and will thrive. But remember, to successfully grow vegetables in roof gardens, you have to water them copiously and frequently. If this sounds like a lot of work, you will forget that once you have your own produce (see list at end of chapter).

PENTHOUSE GARDENS

These lovely areas are rarely seen today; high-rise buildings generally have community garden terraces on the top floor, supervised by building personnel. Still, penthouse apartments with a terrace are occasionally found, and what unique gardens these can be.

The main difference between the smaller roof garden (private

A small pool is the accent of this roof garden balcony with plants beautifully displayed. Container camellias provide grand color. (Photo by Matthew Barr)

home) and the penthouse one is space. Although the same principles govern gardening up high (weight factor and proper selection of trees and shrubs), the design is different for that of the penthouse garden. Along with tubs, boxes, and handsome planters, you must establish a center of interest, or sometimes two areas of accent. A statue and a small water or rock garden are ideal accents. Note, however, that the water garden and the rock garden require care and patience if you want them to yield their bounty of beauty.

A seating area is also almost mandatory to pull the space together. Selection of outdoor furniture is more vital with this garden than with most gardens. The penthouse garden is truly an outdoor room and requires careful selection of tasteful furniture.

Other aspects of penthouse gardening are, as mentioned, the same as for smaller roof gardens.

PLANTS FOR ROOFTOP GARDENS

The following trees and shrubs will withstand wind better than most plants and are suitable for the garden in the air:

TREES
Acer palmatum (Japanese maple)
A. rubrum (red maple)
Albizzia julibrissin (silk tree)
Betula populifolia (gray birch)
Carpinus betulus pryamidalis (pyramidal hornbeam)
Cornus florida (flowering dogwood)
Ginkgo biloba (ginkgo tree)
Koelreuteria paniculata (golden-rain tree)
Laburnum vossi
Malus (flowering crab apple)
Robinia (locust)
Salix babylonica (weeping willow)
Sorbus Aucuparia (mountain ash)

EVERGREEN TREES
Picea abies or *excelsa* (Norway spruce)
Pinus mugo mughus (Mugho pine)
P. Strobus (white pine)
P. sylvestris (Scots pine)
Taxus (yew)

Perennials, annuals, and ivy border this roof garden and the effect is charming in all aspects; rooftop gardening does have immense rewards. (Photo by Matthew Barr)

SHRUBS
Abelia grandiflora (glossy abelia)
Chaenomeles japonica (Japanese quince)
Cotoneaster (cotoneaster)
Euonymus (euonymus)
Forsythia (forsythia)
Ilex (holly)
Ligustrum (privet)
Philadelphus (mock orange)
Pieris japonica (Japanese andromeda)
Pyracantha lalandi (firethorn)
Rhododendron (see Chapter 3)
Rosa
Salix discolor (pussy willow)

VEGETABLES AND HERBS

For years people did not have time to garden the lovely food plants—vegetables and herbs—but now tomatoes and cucumbers, lettuce, and the like are cropping up in the smallest garden, as are herbs. And rightly so. What is more pleasant and more tasty than your own vegetables?

Growing vegetables and herbs is no different from growing perennials and annuals or trees and shrubs. In fact, it may be easier because of new improved varieties, especially the dwarf strains. Remember that vegetables and herbs require abundant amounts of water and sun or they die. On a roof or high-terraced garden, or even on a balcony, you can certainly grow a few boxes with lettuce, radishes, and some herbs. In the ground garden, space or lack of full sun may rule out these plants.

Beets, turnips, lettuce, spinach, and carrots are all good possibilities for the avid city gardener, but no matter what you grow, grow it rapidly and harvest it early. This means providing plenty of rich soil, abundant moisture, and excellent sunlight.

Vegetables like lettuce and peas need cool weather; others, like tomatoes and lima beans, require warmth. Some varieties should be planted before the last frost and others after it. The following chart will guide you:

Vegetable	Buy plants, or seed depth	Warm-season vegetable	Cool-season vegetable	Days from seed to harvest
Bean, lima	1 to 2 inches	X		120
Beet	1 to 2 inches		X	50 to 60
Cabbage	Buy plants		X	60 to 100
Carrots	½ inch		X	70 to 75
Cucumber	1 inch	X		70
Lettuce	½ inch		X	20 to 40
Peppers	Buy plants	X		115
Radish	½ inch		X	20 to 30
Spinach	1 inch		X	60 to 70
Tomato	Buy plants	X		100 to 120

Growing your own herbs is more fun than you may think and generally easier than you anticipate. Home-grown herbs have more flavor and taste than those bought in stores, and there are dozens of herbs that will grow with minimum care. Whether for flavor, fragrance, medicinal teas, or what-have-you, herbs offer many choices.

Most herbs need little space, and even the tiniest garden can accommodate a few kitchen herbs. Furthermore, unlike vegetables, many herbs do not need intense sun or long durations. Two or three hours of sun is fine for most herbs. Grow plants in a well-drained, sandy soil; this is a prime requirement for herbs. Keep the soil evenly moist and thin plants occasionally to keep them in bounds and to prevent them from crowding out other plants.

Herbs can be used directly cut from the plant for salads and seasonings, or they may be dried for future use. The drying process is simple; put leaves and stems on a baking tin in a 200-degree oven with the door open. When dry, strip the leaves and put them in airtight containers. Or dry herbs by hanging them in bunches from the ceiling in an attic or other dark but dry place until it is time to use them.

Sage, tarragon, thyme, basil, parsley, savory, and chives are the easiest herbs to grow under most conditions. Start annual herbs from seed; buy started plants of perennial herbs at nurseries and set them in soil. Plant basil, chives, parsley, rosemary, sage, and thyme after the last frost, ¼ inch deep.

5. The Tenant Gardener ✍

People who like to garden but must lease apartments face a double dilemma. Where do you find that prized garden apartment (is it available to all?) or that garden on the roof? And once it is found, just how much money do you want to invest to install a garden on someone else's property? Expense must be considered when you get ready to sign a long- or short-term lease.

If you see possibilities in a yard, even though it is in sorry shape from neglect, ask the landlord if he is willing to meet you halfway in putting in a garden. The worse he can do is say no.

What To Look For

The apartment hunter seeking a garden apartment should watch for the following things; they will tell him just how successful the garden will be. First, beware of "garden apartments" advertised by real estate agents. This term can include anything from a compound of twelve apartments surrounding a tree to an apartment with an alley corner or postage-stamp-sized backyard.

Once you find a suitable apartment with a backyard, survey it closely. Just how much sunshine will the garden receive daily? If there are high buildings immediately to the east of your building, sun and air circulation will be cut off. Remember that to have flowers, a lawn, or flowering shrubs you need at least three to four hours of daily sunshine, and preferably morning sun, which results from a southern or southeastern exposure. If, however, the exposure is northern and the apartment is just too good to miss, do not give

This garden terrace incorporates a work center in its plan and gives the tenant gardener a great place to work with plants. (Photo by Matthew Barr)

it up. Consider the whole thing a challenge and start planning an all-green garden or a Japanese-style rock garden. Both are beautiful pictures when properly assembled.

Check the soil in the garden area. If it is dry, and caked, it is spent and without nutrition. Usually you have to invest several hundred dollars for fresh topsoil if you want any kind of plant to grow. A 10- x 20-foot area can need 10 or 12 yards of topsoil, and at an average of $7.85 a square yard this can run into money.

57

Fences, doors, and gates to the yard area should also be investigated. Just what condition are they in? Can you use them at all? How much money and time will it take to put them into workable order? When looking at fences and exposures, look up at the rest of the building. How many apartments are above you? What about smoke or soot from nearby chimneys? Air pollution has to be reckoned with, because some plants react adversely to it. If pollution is a problem in your section of the city, you may have to settle for fewer plants and those that will tolerate conditions.

THE AVERAGE BACKYARD GARDEN

If you are getting the typical city backyard that dates from the early 1900s you will probably have an oblong or square central bed, such as I had when I rented an apartment in Chicago. This central bed usually has a lawn in the center and straight concrete walks around it, with narrow borders. That's about it! In its day this was considered a neat and proper town garden.

The rear of this apartment offers a quaint garden spot; container plants against the wall are a prime asset. (Photo by Matthew Barr)

A garden apartment with a fine garden, tough to find in the city but not impossible to have. Plantings are at a minimum and yet the picture is pleasing. (Photo by Molly Adams)

Today we lean more toward the informal type of garden, where there is freedom of personal choice and no strict guidelines to follow. A garden should be personal and relate to the house. Its use is of prime importance, too. Is it merely a lovely green picture to view, or are you going to use it for a retreat and a place to relax in?

Just what exists in the garden now—a few trees, some shrubs? Can you use them as a starting point, or will a completely new garden have to be installed? If so, it will cost you a fortune. If you

59

A handsome backyard garden beautifully landscaped is part of this city site; flowers and trees are beautifully coordinated. (Photo by Hedrich Blessing. Designer: Ben Baldwin, AID)

have a short-term lease, use a few seasonal pot plants instead. Container gardens can be a delight to the eye when properly done. If you have a long-term lease and want to start reconditioning the soil and striving for that very pleasant garden, ask your landlord if he will be willing to share the expense of beautifying his property.

Balcony Gardens

The advent of the modern high-rise building introduced the phenomenon called the balcony or terrace. This is generally a tile or concrete slab installed to soften the blow of a concrete vault. Such areas can be pleasant places for a few plants, but they rarely ever become gardens. Generally they are small, windy, and exceedingly difficult to cope with. If you look at them first for what they are,

Narrow but nice is this fine backyard garden; mosses and ground covers, hanging plants, and container plants are part of the landscape. (Photo by Matthew Barr)

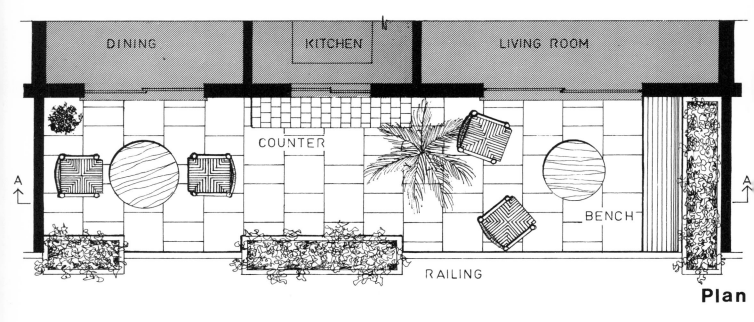

DINING   KITCHEN   LIVING ROOM

A

COUNTER

BENCH

RAILING

Plan

Section A-A

Elevation

Balcony garden. (Drawing by Adrian Martinez)

A typical city balcony situation; evergreens are used predominantly in the concealed boxes to provide a lush scene from within and from outside the apartment.
(Drawing by Charles Hoeppner)

you will not suffer disillusionment later. They will accommodate a few pot plants and perhaps a tree.

The balcony should not be confused with the balcony terraces or roof gardens found in older apartment houses; these can indeed be handsome areas where you can design and garden to your heart's content. These are available, but not as plentifully (see Chapter 4).

Balconies are usually narrow and long and provide little space for plants. Still, as mentioned, with clever planning some plants can be grown. Have enough plants to please the eye, but not so many that you end up with a jungle that you can't walk through.

On the balcony, put plants in ornamental containers. Use vines and trailers in wooden planters, to cover bare walls and railings or to give you privacy from nearby neighbors. Use seasonal flowering plants for color; they are available at most florists. Do not use one large pot; group several small ones together for a lush display. Don't forget trailing plants in hanging baskets for added decoration. Even a pair of lovely *Asparagus sprengeri* adds a note of lacy loveliness to an area, and at eye level such plants are impressive sights.

Grow vines flat against a wall or on a trellis in espalier fashion to conserve space and yet bring leafy green into the picture. Vines may take more care than most plants—pruning and trimming—but they are still worth every effort. And they cover a multitude of sins without taking up too much space.

Window boxes of plants are frequently seen on balconies, and these are fine if they are sturdily constructed and securely anchored in place. Don't just suspend them from railings without adequate support. Put window boxes *within* the perimeter of the balcony, never hanging in mid air (see also Chapter 7).

In winter, bring most plants indoors, unless you have evergreens. Container plants at a bright window or in any area where they have some light and cooler temperatures can then decorate the home.

Don't leave balconies bare. With only a few plants they can become welcome retreats rather than merely additional space.

6. Making the Garden Grow

The amount of work necessary to maintain your city garden depends on the garden's size and design. If a simple plan is followed—a few trees and shrubs—minimum care is all that is required. If your garden is somewhat elaborate, you will need more time and energy. However, the rewards are vast.

No matter what the size of your garden or what you are growing, good soil is essential. Containers such as planters and raised beds are other prime requirements for successful city gardens. If you start right, later care will be reduced. And, finally, a careful selection of plants that can tolerate some neglect if necessary and still survive is wisest. Feeding and watering are important, too, as are pruning and keeping insects out of the garden.

Soil

To adequately support plant life, soil should be fertile and have the proper consistency. It must be porous in texture so water and air can enter, and it must be rich in nutrients so plants can grow.

Soil in city yards is rarely adequate to support plant life. Usually, it has not been worked for years and is drained of nutrients. But too often the comment that nothing will grow in the city is completely wrong; if the soil is good, plants *will* grow.

In new properties conditions may be even worse. Builders often strip the essential topsoil from the site and the ground is compacted by heavy machinery. Little if anything will grow in a subsoil base.

No matter what the condition of the soil in the city garden, there

Soil being spaded to be later mixed with top soil and humus to provide a rich friable soil for the garden. (USDA photo)

will be evidence of a distinctly darker upper layer that was once rich and friable. This is the topsoil. Under this will be the subsoil; this layer of earth must be reworked before anything else is done. Dig down about 12 inches and work the soil with spade and hoe until it is friable. Now condition the soil. Add humus, maintaining the right proportions if you want good plant growth. Humus—animal manure, compost, leafmold—is decayed organic matter; that is, rotted, once-living organisms. Humus provides soil with body and serves as food for plants and microorganisms, so it must be replaced.

You must decide yourself how much humus to add to soil. Your decision should be based on what plants you want to grow and on the amount of humus now present in the soil. I have found a mixture of about 1 inch of compost to about 6 inches of soil very satisfactory.

You must also use fertilizers in the soil because they contain nitrogen, phosphorous, and potassium (potash), all essential to healthy plant growth.

A good soil allows moisture to pass quickly through pores (which carry away excess water) to reach a plant's roots; there it is stored for future use. Soil must never be allowed to become water-logged; if it does, air will not circulate freely, and the plant's growth will be affected.

Good drainage of soil is absolutely necessary; otherwise the roots of plants get shallow and die because they cannot reach down for the stored water. Poor drainage is common to most soils and is usually caused by a layer of hard earth.

Soil must be porous so plant roots can get oxygen. It should be crumbly and of an open texture for perfect air and water circulation. (Air enters with the water that drains through the soil.) You can improve the soil's physical structure by turning it, keeping it porous, and using composts and mulches year round. Remember that porosity is the key to good soil.

Good soil is porous, high in organic matter, crumbly and easily broken apart. The soil tilth is excellent so air and water can move through the soil easily. (USDA photo)

You can buy new soil by the truckload from building-supply yards or garden centers, generally a 6- or 8-cubic-foot load. Soil is available in various grades; the best is screened and already has fertilizer. This type is the most expensive. Lower-grade soils are not screened and cost a little less, and there are some soils (which are actually "fills" and nothing more than subsoils) that can be purchased for as little as $2.85 a yard. Buy the best soil you can possibly afford because it will pay off in a bountiful harvest of flowers rather than a scanty yield. Soil delivered in trucks is dumped at your property; you must do the hauling and spreading, which is not as easy as it sounds.

Soil is also available by the bushel from local nurseries. This is excellent all-purpose soil ready for the garden and can be used if you do not need too much. Soils packaged in 50- and 100-pound bags are also satisfactory but generally more expensive than soil bought by the truckload.

pH Symbol

The pH scale measures the acidity or alkalinity of soil. Soil with a pH of 7 is neutral; below 7 the soil is acid, and above 7 it is alkaline. You should know the pH of your soil so that you can get the maximum use from all fertilizers supplied to it. To determine the pH, have it tested by state agricultural authorities or do your own test, using one of the commercial kits.

Most trees and shrubs prefer a more or less neutral soil (between 6 and 7), although there are a few exceptions. In alkaline soils, potash becomes less effective and eventually is locked in. In very acid soils, the aluminum becomes so active that it is toxic to plants. Acidity in soil controls many functions: it determines the availability of the food in the soil, governs which bacteria will thrive in it, and somewhat affects the rate at which roots can take up moisture and leaves manufacture food.

To lower the pH of soil (increase the acidity), apply ground sulfur: 1 pound per 100 square feet. This lowers the pH of loam soil about one point. Spread the sulfur on top of the soil and then apply water.

To raise (sweeten) the pH of soil, add ground limestone: 10 pounds per 150 square feet. Scatter it on the soil or mix it well with the top few inches of soil and water. Add ground limestone or hydrated lime in several applications at six- or eight-week intervals rather than using a lot at one time.

SOIL CONDITIONERS

Peat moss is a soil conditioner, not a fertilizer. It holds moisture like a sponge and is useful when added to claylike soil because it aerates it and allows oxygen to reach plant roots. In large quantities it has a slightly acid tendency. Add one-third quantity of peat moss to one-third new soil for your yard; dig and fork it into the soil.

Leafmold is high in fertilizer value and an excellent soil conditioner; it furnishes nutrients in their most natural form. You can collect leafmold from woods or buy it in bales from nurseries. It lightens any heavy soil and can be used in equal parts with topsoil.

Compost is a real tonic for plants. This decayed vegetable matter—grass cuttings, vegetable tops, rakings—is what good soil is made of. It is enriched with manure and fertilizers and is an essential soil additive.

WATERING

In summer months it is difficult to water plants too much. There are few plants that really enjoy being dry. Cacti and some succulents

Transplanting is done with additional compost; note the plant is placed with root ball intact. (USDA photo)

Compost piles are difficult to have in the city but they are invaluable to provide essential organic matter to soils. (USDA photo)

that can withstand drought if necessary still need good moisture to thrive. Most garden plants need a steady supply of moisture in the ground; without it they quickly succumb.

Because city plants are not growing in optimum conditions, watering is quite important. In cities, plants must exist between walls and fences, walks and concrete, and often in shallow soil; moisture that would descend in the form of dew in the country is absorbed in the atmosphere before reaching city ground. Reflected heat from concrete buildings further intensifies arid conditions.

When to water depends on variable factors, but just how much to water is easy to decide: water thoroughly and deeply. It takes water almost one hour to penetrate about 40 inches of soil. Thus, if you are watering for ten minutes hardly any of the plant roots are getting moisture. If you keep only the top of the soil wet with scanty water-

70

ings, roots have to reach up instead of down; the result is a shallow-rooted plant that rarely fares well. To ensure a healthy plant, roots must work deep into the soil to seek out moisture.

Although it is important to water thoroughly and deeply, you do not want to cause an overwatered condition—a flooding of the soil—for then the supply of oxygen to the roots is blocked and plants start to drown. Allow enough time between waterings for complete moisture absorption by soil and plants. This is the tricky part of watering: not *how much*, but *how much when*. This will depend on such variables as wind, temperature, light intensity, soil, and rainfall.

Watering is important for all plants, but it is vital to newly transplanted ones and seedlings; these really need copious amounts of

Watering plants with a home garden sprinkler saves time and worry. There are many sprinklers at nurseries. (USDA photo)

water to get them growing. If you allow them to become dry for even a day you may harm the plants seriously, particularly in hot weather. After the first few critical weeks you can develop a regular watering schedule.

Plants in boxes and containers in rooftop situations need even more frequent watering than plants in the ground. During dry, hot months, soil in containers dries out more quickly than you think, and plants may need water twice a day (evaporation is more rapid than from open ground).

Air pollution, soot, oil, and dust cause plant leaves to become clogged. Plants breathe through their minute pores, so you must wash and hose the foliage of city plants. In fact, many plants that do not

An everpresent weed is the dandelion. (USDA photo)

Another bothersome weed is dock. (USDA photo)

ordinarily succeed in city gardens can be given longer life with frequent washings. Not only will washing keep plants healthy, but it will keep them looking better. A strong but fine mist from the hose early in the morning a few times a week does wonders for city plants.

Washing not only applies to perennials and deciduous plants, but also to conifers and evergreens. In spring, these plants really need a good washing to rid them of city soot accumulations. Use a mild soap-and-water solution and take a soft brush (or even a sponge) to the leaves. Rinse plants thoroughly so they are shiny clean.

73

PRUNING

If the city garden is allowed to grow out of control, it will look un-kempt. Country gardens can, to some extent, be neglected and al-lowed to grow in a natural state, but this is not so with city gardens. Prune any tree with dead wood; if the tree is too large for you to handle, call in a tree service.

Pruning is often neglected but it should not be, because it en-courages bushiness instead of spindly growth; cleans out winterkill

Prune trees yearly to help them grow; then apply tree-wound paint. (True-temper Products photo)

branches, which are eyesores; and encourages flowers and sturdier wood. Although pruning is generally done in spring, broken and dead wood should be removed regardless of the season. Early spring-flowering shrubs like forsythia, however, should not be pruned until after they bloom.

Shrubs that bloom later should have annual pruning, according to species and variety, sometime in spring. Rose pruning depends on the type of rose being grown. Cut hybrid teas to within 4 inches off the ground. Prune bushy roses less; cut back to about one-third of the natural growth. With rambling roses, clean out dead wood and treat the plants like early-blooming shrubs. Do the main pruning after bloom; then cut to the ground.

Most conifers and evergreens need little pruning; hemlock and yew, for example, require just an occasional clipping.

Pruning methods vary, but generally you prune from the inside of the plant outward and from the bottom up. "Top-lighting" fruit trees or shrubs means opening the center of the tree to allow in more light and air. Take out crossing branches and branches of lesser value. Cut them cleanly at the trunk or the first strong crotch and do not leave stubs—these become infected. It is vital to know where to make a cut when pruning; haphazard cutting must be avoided. Make a cut only above a bud, small side branch, or main branch. Cut branches in the direction you want the new growth to take.

WEEDING AND GROOMING

Weeding is a necessary evil in the garden, but it need not be so unpleasant if it is done a few times a week rather than once a month. It is important to get rid of weeds because they rob plants of nutrition and eventually will take over. May and June are prime weeding months.

When annuals start to look straggly in midsummer, cut them back to about half their height to give them a fresh start. All annual seedlings should be pinched back while they are small to encourage bushiness and side branching. Petunias, zinnias, and marigolds in particular need this treatment.

After the first killing frost, discard all annuals and cut perennials to the ground. Remove all leaves, stems, and garden rubbish.

Fertilizers

Because the nutrients in soils are absorbed rapidly by plants, fertilizers must be used. Annuals and other flowering plants especially need feeding to make them yield a harvest of blooms. From early June to September fertilize new plants every two weeks. Use fertilizers more frequently but in smaller quantities on shrubs and woody plants; infrequent feeding with large doses of fertilizers can injure plants. Do not feed shrubs and woody plants after August or you will encourage soft growth, which will be susceptible to cold weather.

The three most important elements necessary for plant growth are

Removing unwanted branches from trees is important, and this handy saw makes it easy. (True-temper Products photo)

nitrogen, phosphorus, and potash. These are most likely to be deficient in cultivated soils.

Nitrogen stimulates vegetative development and is necessary for healthy stem and leaf growth. Phosphorus is needed in all phases of plant growth, and potash promotes the general vigor of a plant by making it resistant to certain diseases. It also has a balancing influence on other plant nutrients. Various trace elements such as copper, iron, sulfur, zinc, and manganese are also important.

To feed shrubs, vines, flowers, and vegetables, spread fertilizer on the ground around the plant and then water thoroughly to dissolve the fertilizer.

Today there are many plant foods, but basically most have nitrogen, phosphorus, potash, and some trace elements. Contents are on the package or the bottle, marked in numbers. The first numeral is the percentage of nitrogen; the second, of phosphorus, and the third, of potash.

Fertilizers are offered in five forms:
> POWDERED: Good, but blows away on a windy day.
> CONCENTRATED LIQUIDS: Used for all fertilizing.
> CONCENTRATED POWDERS: Diluted in water and applied to foliage or roots.
> CONCENTRATED TABLETS: Used mainly for house plants.
> PELLETED OR GRANULAR: Most popular; easy to spread. Add water after spreading.

In addition to these man-made fertilizers, there are nitrogen materials that help plants grow. These include organic matter such as animal and vegetable tankage, manures, and cottonseed and other meals and ureaform compounds, which are synthetic materials made by a chemical union of urea and formaldehyde. Do not confuse urea (quickly available nitrogen) with ureaform.

There are also fertilizers for specific plants. Because there are so many plant foods, know which ones will do what for your garden. For example, on lawns use a high nitrogen food like 20-20-10. For flower beds and plant blooms select a food with a high phosphorus content like 12-12-12. If you need something to improve soil structure and release nutrients slowly, choose an organic food like blood meal or bone meal (available in packages at nurseries).

7. Planters and Containers

Whether you have a rooftop or a backyard garden, you will most likely be doing a great deal of gardening in planters and boxes, tubs and pots. Container gardening offers a world of advantages, and sometimes for the renter it is the only way to have a garden without excessive cost since most container plantings can be moved when you move.

Whether they are made of wood or masonry, planters offer a freedom of design in the garden that brings shapes and forms into being, and this, of course, is the way to make the garden lively and interesting. The planter garden is never monotonous or unattractive because geometric shapes can be arranged in many ways to create eye interest. Naturally, not all the garden will be in planters. Use a combination of ground plantings, pot gardens, and planters to provide an attractive picture.

At one time tubs and boxes were seldom available commercially, but today there are many kinds sold at stores and nurseries. Whether you make your own or buy them, containers are ideal for all kinds of plants, and a few decorative tubs on the rooftop or in the backyard can transform the ordinary site into an extraordinary one.

PERMANENT PLANTERS

These planters are generally built to fill a specific place. They can be rectangular, square, triangular, or circular, and made of wood, masonry, brick, or concrete. No matter where they are used they are highly decorative, and they have advantages over gardening in the ground.

78

This city garden uses container plants for beauty; the elegant fountain is a focal point, and small-leaved vines complete the picture. (Drawing by Charles Hoeppner)

Raised planter beds make bending easier and provide growing areas with excellent drainage. The walls of the planters also keep out greedy roots from nearby trees and invasive weeds. Furthermore, the raised planter bed makes the flowers and foliage appear more decorative and brings plants closer to eye level.

79

Even a few container plants bring beauty to a corner; once again, vines are used to provide vertical accent. (Drawings by Charles Hoeppner)

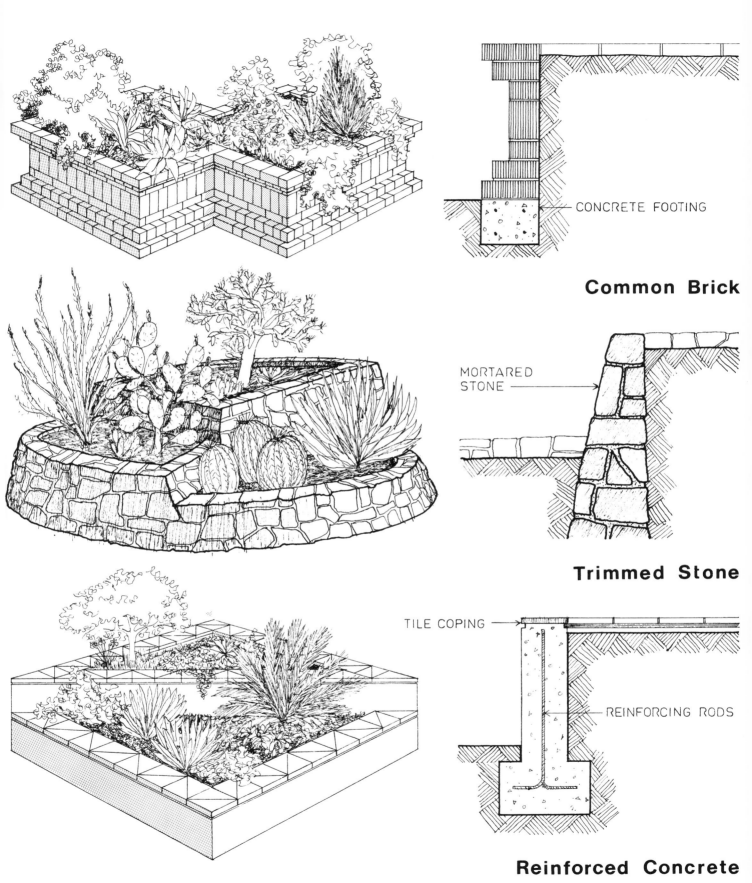

Common Brick

CONCRETE FOOTING

MORTARED STONE

Trimmed Stone

TILE COPING

REINFORCING RODS

Reinforced Concrete

Permanent masonry planters. (Drawing by Adrian Martinez)

These geometric wooden planters add a great deal to a garden; they have been painted to dramatize their lines but can also be used unpainted. Almost any plant can be grown in a planter. (Photo by Ken Molino)

Although masonry units are excellent for gardens, wooden planters are perhaps more popular. Wood is a natural material that looks good in the garden, and you can easily make wooden planters, even if you are not an expert carpenter.

WOODEN PLANTERS

To fill a specific area you will have to make your own planters or have them made at local woodworking shops. Be sure to use durable

Wooden planters are part of this newly started city garden; the simple straight lines are pleasing to the eye. (Photo by Ken Molino)

woods such as redwood and cypress; they can withstand the rigors of the weather. Other woods are satisfactory, but they must be treated with wood preservative to prevent their rapid deterioration.

There are many kinds of planter boxes you can make and several methods of construction. All boxes are generally made the same way, but we have found 2- x 12-foot redwood boards, 2 inches thick, excellent for outdoor planters. Cut boards to the desired length and nail and screw all corners. Space the bottom boards ¼ to ½ inch

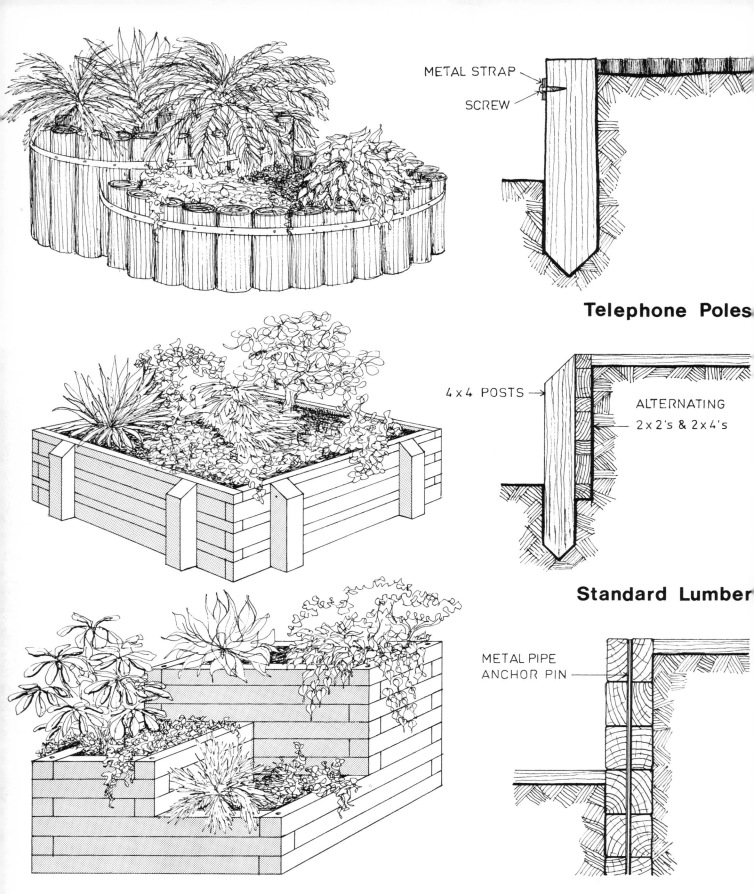

Telephone Poles

METAL STRAP

SCREW

Standard Lumber

4 x 4 POSTS

ALTERNATING
2 x 2's & 2 x 4's

Railroad Ties

METAL PIPE
ANCHOR PIN

Permanent wooden planters. (Drawing by Adrian Martinez)

apart and use small wooden cleats as supports for the planter. The cleats elevate the box, eliminate hiding places for insects, and permit air circulation under the box for better plant growth and drainage. Elevated planters also look better than those set flush on the ground.

Planters should be at least 30 inches deep and 14 inches wide to accommodate plants; any length can be used.

Modular boxes are rarely as long as planters; their proportions are generally in modules of 8 inches: 8 x 8, 8 x 16, 8 x 24, 8 x 32,

This city garden depends on the circular pattern of the brick set off by stepped wooden planters. It is an unusual arrangement but comes off beautifully. (Photo by Matthew Barr)

8 x 40, and so on. Any of these boxes used by itself is fine, but combine it with other boxes and you achieve a variety of geometric patterns. Stack boxes in a grid effect or in any number of ways to provide handsome designs. Modular boxes are especially effective for demarcation of property lines or on rooftop areas.

Triangular and hexagonal boxes are other ideas for planters and these, too, can be used in many different patterns—for example, a group of eight together, in tandem, or in a stacked arrangement.

Rather than spacing bottom boards for drainage of water in smaller boxes, install ½-inch holes in the bottom so excess water can escape.

Planting the boxes is easy: install curved pieces of pot shards over the drainage holes to prevent soil from washing away when plants are watered. Put in at least 1 inch of pea gravel and some charcoal granules to keep the soil sweet. Add soil and put in plants; keep the soil line at least 1 inch below the top of the box to allow space for watering.

Window Boxes

Window boxes have been sorely neglected in this country, but in Europe they are frequently filled with plants to add beauty to a house.

While many materials are now being used for boxes—plastic, metal, concrete—the old-fashioned window box is my choice. Select redwood if possible, for it weathers well and resists decay for many years. Other woods will need preservatives (available at hardware stores). Beware of very long window boxes; filled with soil they become very heavy and hanging them can be a problem. If your window is large, use two small boxes rather than one large one. The most satisfactory sizes are 28 to 36 inches long, 10 inches wide and 12 inches deep.

Bolt window boxes to wall studs and install sturdy L-shaped iron brackets to support them. You can put pot plants in the box and camouflage the tops with moss or you can plant directly into the box. You can make your own window boxes or buy commercial ones. Whatever you decide, window-box gardening is really a boon for the city dweller and plants grow well in them. They are exposed to air circulation on all sides, benefit from rain, and have good light.

Some excellent plants for window boxes include: geraniums, lantanas, lobelias, nasturtiums, petunias, impatiens, achimenes, and fuchsias.

Old-fashioned window boxes are charming in almost any situation and here pro-vide a decorative note to a city house. (Drawing by Charles Hoeppner)

Brick planters do the job in this garden and they are indeed effective. Brick harmonizes well with almost all plantings. (Photo by Matthew Barr)

A small container garden adds charm to a balcony corner. (Photo by Matthew Barr)

Masonry Planters

When planning your planter, study the site carefully so the planters become an integral part of the design. Filled with plants, they will screen an unsightly corner near a house wall and provide a tie-in between the house and garden. Further they camouflage bare walls and straight lines which are hardly pleasing.

Planters, whether geometrical or oval, break the monotony of the usual rectangular site and provide eye interest; on rooftop gardens they are indispensable not only as places for plants but as dividers and islands to guide traffic.

A decorative stone urn is the focal point of this small garden area. (Photo by Matthew Barr)

For a masonry planter, lay out a string in a straight line on the ground and dig a trench 6 to 12 inches deep along this line; make the trench 3 to 4 inches wider than the masonry wall you are planning. Fill the trench with a ready-to-mix concrete, or, if you prefer to mix your own, use 1 part cement, 3 parts sand, and 5 parts gravel. The foundation or footing should be below the frost line. This varies from state to state, check with your local building department.

16"

16"

tongue & groove

12"

2"

PLAN

SECTION

Redwood

18"

18"

18"

2 x 4's cap

16"

2 x 2's

PLAN

SECTION

Cedar Shingles

9"

20"

12"

metal channels

8 x 8 tiles

metal base

PLAN

SECTION

Quarry Tile

Portable planters. (Drawing by Adrian Martinez)

When the footing is dry, lay stones or bricks on it, putting them in place with mortar; use a level on each brick or building block so the wall will be even. Ready-to-mix mortar is fine, or you can make mortar with 1 part cement, 3 parts sand, and some lime. If you are using irregularly shaped stones like cobblestone or fieldstone, strive for a handsome pattern by using large and small stones in a design. Remember to provide drainpipes at the bottom of the wall to carry away excess water.

When the wall is the height you want, trim it with a cap of flagstone strips or concrete.

TUBS AND BOXES

Like planters, boxes come in an infinite number of designs. The container with flared or tapered sides is attractive and a good housing for annuals or bulbs. An 18-inch top tapering to a 10-inch base is a good size for most arrangements. Use 1-inch-thick redwood or cedar, and miter corners if possible. Use a small, 1-inch moulding as a pedestal to give the box a finished look.

Cube boxes are effective for small trees and shrubs. I use 2- x 12-inch redwood for a 24-inch box; it seems ideal for the size of plants necessary in a small yard. To give the box a finished appearance, stain the wood a dark color and then nail 1- x 1-inch wooden strips around it spaced ½ inch apart.

Concrete tubs can also be a do-it-yourself project. You will need wood framing for the size of the box and a concrete mix that is fairly stiff: 3 parts cement, 1 part sand, and 2 parts stones. Or use Sakrete commercial mix and just add water. Pour the mix into the form, put a presoaked standard clay pot in position, and fill in and around it with concrete to the top of the frame. When the concrete is firm, scrub it with a wire brush; twenty-four hours later, remove the wooden forms and take out the pot. Run water over the surface and scrub it with a wire brush.

If time is at a premium (and it usually is), you can buy all kinds of concrete tubs and wooden boxes at nurseries and florist shops.

8. Shopping for Plants

In the city, shopping for and buying healthy plants may be as important as growing them well. Of course, you can drive to a nursery in the country, but this is not always practical, and if you buy many plants it is difficult to transport them, unless you have a station wagon. However, in large cities there are florist-greenhouses; these are your best bet for most plants because they will deliver plants and can give you on-the-spot advice about which plants will succeed in your area.

Mail-order suppliers are another excellent source for plants, and today, because of air shipment, getting them to you is no problem. Furthermore, most mail-order specialists know how to pack and ship plants so they arrive in good condition.

Local florists within the downtown district of a large city are other sources of plants, and seasonal perennials and annuals are occasionally available there, as are gift plants of fine quality.

Companies such as Terrestris in New York and the Greenhouse in Chicago are still other fine sources for tubbed trees and shrubs. Prices may be high, but quality is assured.

SELECTING PLANTS

One of the main problems when buying plants is that few people know how to differentiate between a healthy one and a sick one. The surest way to get first-rate material is to deal with reputable nurserymen and dealers. But if this is your first purchase, just how are you to know whom you are dealing with and what you are getting? Most companies are reputable and try to handle first-class merchandise, but remember that the man you buy from has not grown the plants. They come from large commercial growers and then go through a distributor before they get to your city dealer. In such an exchange, the chance for human error is increased and some plants are bound to suffer.

Once a plant leaves a nurseryman it is yours. Most nurserymen will guarantee a plant's name, color, and variety, but that is all; the rest is up to you. Remember to get names of plants; it will be easier for state agricultural services and horticulturists to help you if you have questions about the plant later.

How do you tell a good plant from a bad one? There are several things to look for to ensure your getting a healthy plant. First, inspect the plant for insects; most common garden pests such as aphids, mealy bugs, or scale are easily seen. Especially scrutinize the bottoms of leaves and branch axils, for this is where these culprits generally gather.

A great many plants come in cans ready for garden planting. (Photo by Joyce Wilson)

Dusty and soot-covered leaves may indicate that a plant has been in the nursery a long time, in which case it is probably not too robust. Wan growth (limp stems) is another indication that a plant is not up to par. Of course, it may just be a lack of water, but why buy a plant that has been water starved for days? Plants in caked soil are rarely a good buy either; generally, they have been at the florist's a long time. Soil is spent, and the plant has been without nutrients for some time and is not too robust.

Because potted plants and seedlings constitute a good part of city gardens you must really use good sense when buying them. In large garden centers and nurseries, plants are usually put out for fast seasonal sale, and the nurseryman rarely has time to water or keep them properly. This is not a comment against the seller; it is merely a condition that exists. Flats of seedling annuals will be different in size and appearance: some will be perky and healthy, while others of the same variety will be wan and limp. Seedlings in flats should be bushy, not crowded. Bedding plants and perennials may be in flats or in pots of various sizes. Once again, look for the plant that is bushy and stocky. Sometimes potted perennials are a better buy than seedling flats because the shock of transplanting is lessened with container plants.

Avoid bargain plants; they rarely deliver what the advertisements promise. Since you are investing money in soil, containers, and your time, buy only top-quality plants for satisfaction. Bargain plants are generally inferior, and although experienced gardeners may coax them back to health, they are a waste of money for the novice.

In selecting trees and shrubs, balled-and-burlapped (B and B) ones or trees in cans are better than bare-rooted dormant stock. They are more expensive than the latter, but they have a much better chance of succeeding in the city garden. Dormant plants take longer before they start to grow, sometimes city conditions are not good enough to put them into growth, and often they do not look their best the first year. For trees, shrubs, and plants, whenever possible go to the nursery where they are growing. Not only are you able to see exactly what you are getting, but you can ask the nurseryman any questions you may have about the plants.

Plants in flats—shallow wooden or plastic boxes—are most economical. Annuals, perennials, and ground covers are sold this way.

1 CUT OUT PLANTS IN SQUARES W/KNIFE OR TROWEL

Plants in Flats

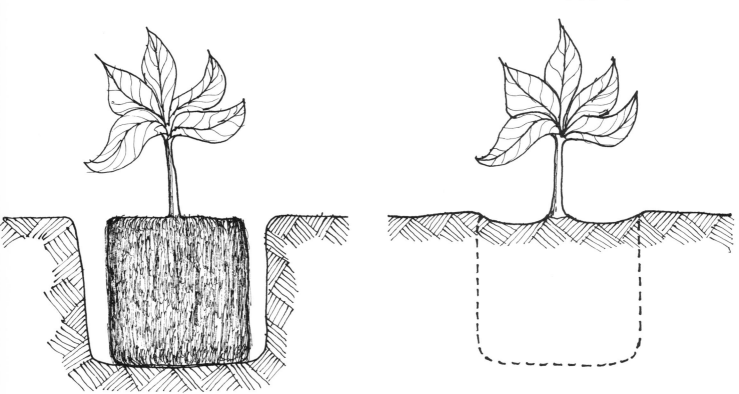

2 GENTLY PLACE IN HOLE (DON'T FORCE IN)

3 FIRM SOIL & MAKE DEPRESSION FOR WATER

Planting from flats. (Drawing by Adrian Martinez)

There may be twelve, twenty-four, or thirty small plants to a flat, depending on the variety, and these seedlings are ready for planting in the ground. With plants in flats rather than in containers, even if you lose a few the odds in terms of money are in your favor.

Generally, nurseries in your locale sell trees and shrubs that are suitable for your climate, so you probably won't have to check weather-zone garden maps to see if a plant will grow in your garden. If it is at your local nursery, chances are it is a hardy plant for your area and a plant that is known to grow well in your locale.

When buying from mail-order catalogs, read descriptions so you know what you are getting. There are many varieties of *Euonymus* or *Weigela*—improved varieties made possible by extensive hybridization to bring you the very best plant—so why not get these rather than inferior kinds? These varieties are either denoted by capital letters or single quotation marks, for example, *Weigela* 'Bristol Ruby.' Pay attention to the varieties that the catalogs say are improved, and if possible, try to fit them into your garden plan.

Do not be afraid of mail-order buying; as mentioned, most nurseries are reliable and know how to ship plants so they arrive in tip-top shape.

Annuals and perennials are offered in flats or in small pots as shown. (Photo by Joyce Wilson)

GETTING PLANTS READY FOR THE GARDEN

Once plants are delivered or you have brought them home, water them well. The best policy is to get shrubs and trees in the ground as soon as possible; if they are in cans you have to cut the cans yourself or have it done at nurseries when you purchase plants. Seedlings, shrubs, bare-rooted stock, and balled-and-burlapped stock should all

Trained espaliers are ready at nurseries for planting. (Photo by Joyce Wilson)

go into the ground as soon as possible. If you must leave them for a day or so, be sure they are in a somewhat shady place and keep them moist.

Do not panic if plants appear somewhat limp the first few weeks after you have transplanted them. It takes time for them to adjust to new conditions, and it is especially true that during this time they are more subject to harm from over- or under-watering, too much or not enough light, and so on. These plants are like small children and so must be carefully tended during the first few weeks they are with you. Once they are established they require minimum maintenance. Thus, buy plants at the time of year you can give them some attention.

Help!

If plants have been with you a few months and they are still not growing or responding, or if you have had plants for years and suddenly they start to fail, do not let them perish. There are many places you can seek help. First read a good standard outdoor-gardening book to see if you can determine the ailment. If this does not help you, there are other courses to follow, and by all means do seek them out. These are services provided by your state and federal government, and since you are paying for them, use them!

The United States Department of Agriculture publishes many booklets and pamphlets about specific plants—shrubs, trees, and so on. These are available for the asking from the Department of Agriculture, Washington, D.C. If there is not time to wait for replies, call the local state agricultural extension service; these services are generally affiliated with colleges throughout the country. This extension service is your own private answering service as a taxpayer. It can answer questions about plants, improving soil, and fighting insects.

Horticultural societies in large cities are other places where you can get answers about plants. However, you must be a member; but if you are, the rewards are vast. Their libraries are at your service, and there are competent people at the offices to answer gardening questions. Check your city phone book for specific horticultural societies.

9. Plant Material and How To Use It

In the country you can do some experimenting with plants, putting them here and there and if they don't succeed in a spot, moving them. In the city, proper selection of plant material and where it goes is necessary because the city gardener doesn't have the time to test, nor does he want the additional expense of bringing in more soil. Study the sun and shade and wind idiosyncrasies of your site and choose plants that are appropriate for your conditions.

Avoid hit-and-miss gardening because, as mentioned, having soil delivered is expensive and difficult and moving plants unnecessarily weakens them further.

Sun Orientation

It takes but a few days to determine whether your garden is sunny, half shaded, or fully shaded. Indeed, just how much sunlight your property gets may be a deciding factor in purchasing a plant. Note where the sun is at a particular time of day; then it is easy to buy appropriate plants for your individual conditions.

Morning sun is preferable for such plants as vegetables, herbs, and annuals; in fact, you can't grow these plants without it. Afternoon sun is fine for perennials, shrubs, and certain trees. Although the sunny site is best, there are many, many plants for the shady garden. Actually, a garden of green plants has a certain lush beauty that is appealing to many people. And there are many trees and shrubs that will adjust, if not prosper, in the shady garden.

100

TRANSPLANTING

Generally, devote the early spring and late fall to transplanting shrubs, trees, and perennials. When good weather is on the way, the plants have a far better chance of succeeding than they do in inclement weather. Remember to try to order trees, shrubs, and vines balled and burlapped or in cans. These plants have a far better chance of surviving in the city than do bare-rooted dormant plants. In the country, bare-root stock, which is cheaper, is fine because conditions

Leaf size and texture have been given careful consideration in this small garden. The small-leaved plants balance the larger-leaved specimens and fine-textured ground cover accents the scene. (Photo by Ken Molino)

This small city garden is a study in leaf textures and size; the gradation from small-leaved to large-leaved plants provides rhythm and eye appeal. (Photo by Roger Scharmer)

are better. In the city, however, bare-root plants are apt to be a headache and will be more expensive in the long run if you have to replace them.

When planting, be sure the hole is somewhat deeper and wider than the root ball and then refill the excavation with rich topsoil. A good rule of thumb when planting shrubs and trees is to leave 1 foot below the root ball and 1 foot more width on all sides. When the plant is in place, untie the burlap but do not remove it; let it decay naturally so it contributes a bit of humus to the soil. Firm the topsoil in place around the tree, but do not pack it down tightly. Eliminate air pockets in the soil; they prevent roots from making contact with soil and are detrimental to good drainage.

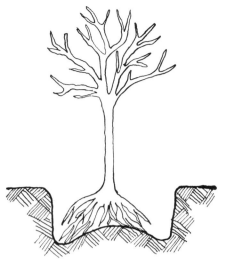

F DRY, SOAK OVERNIGHT

SPREAD ROOTS OVER MOUND

FILL W/SOIL & WATER.

Bare Root

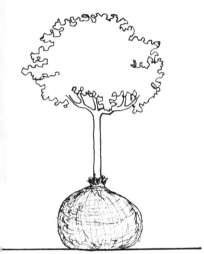
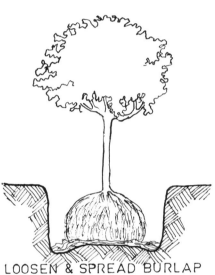

HANDLE CAREFULLY

LOOSEN & SPREAD BURLAP

FILL W/SOIL & WATER

Burlapped

CUT CAN & REMOVE CAREFULLY

LOOSEN SOIL & ROOTS SLIGHTLY

FILL W/SOIL & WATER

Canned

Planting trees. (Drawing by Adrian Martinez)

Prepare the ground so there is a saucer depression around the collar of the plant. Fill this slowly with water, and keep it filled until the whole root ball is saturated. Remember to religiously water the tree or shrub during its first weeks with you. This means slow, deep waterings. If necessary, punch some holes about 20 inches deep around the outside of the planted root ball so water can reach the deeper roots. A pole or crowbar is fine for making the holes.

Textures and Patterns

No garden should just be put together without considering how it will look as a whole. Select plants not only for easy growing and for shade or sun placement but for what they can do in the garden to create an interesting picture.

Study leaf size, texture, and color; some plants are feathery in appearance and others make bold accents. Strive for a pleasing combination of plant materials judiciously placed to delight, not insult the eye. Try to use the gradation scale: small-leaved plants followed by medium-leaved plants and then large, bold foliage to give the garden a sense of rhythm. Or start at the other end of the scale, with large-leaved plants diminishing to small-leaved varieties.

With flowers, choose colors that go well together; for instance, red zinnias next to white flowers are jarring, but red and orange flowers alongside each other are charming.

The All-year Garden

Gardens are meant for four seasons, and here lies the beauty of many plants. In spring, tiny buds and new green shoots are a tonic after winter weather; in summer the bounty of colorful flowers is a spectacular sight; and in fall the changing colors of many trees and shrubs can turn your property into a gold-and-red painted picture. In winter, too, bare branches make handsome sculptures against white snow and city concrete, and evergreens provide essential color.

Remember that since the city garden is very much a part of the home because it is constantly within view, an attractive picture throughout the four seasons is what you want to aim for. Plan ahead for a beautiful all-year garden; it doesn't cost a penny more than a garden good for only a season.

In September, October, and November, lay the foundation for

next year's garden. Plant evergreens for winter color, and get the wonderful perennials into the soil for next summer's flowers. Remember to get bulbs, the first harbingers of spring, into the ground. They can bring so much early color to gardens.

Place evergreens in the background and use deciduous and flowering shrubs closer to the house; in summer they serve as foils for other plants, and in winter, when deciduous plants lose their leaves, the evergreens come forth in all their lovely dark-green colors to keep the garden attractive.

March is the gardener's busy time. Repair such structures as fences, screens, canopies, and so forth. Build planter boxes and check tools to be sure you will have equipment on hand when needed. This is the

Trees are beautifully chosen here to give this garden immense eye appeal and beauty. The mass of plantings at the rear balances the picture. (Photo by Ken Molino)

Another example of intelligent landscaping is this handsome front yard garden; everything in it is adroitly coordinated to make a stunning picture. (Photo by Matthew Barr)

time to plant dormant trees and shrubs and to turn soil as soon as it is workable. Newly planted material should be mulched with peat moss or other mulches. If you have a basement or a garage where temperatures can be maintained, start slow-growing annuals to get a head start on spring.

Deciduous trees and shrubs need a light feeding now, and broadleafed evergreens can be pruned; remove dead or damaged wood.

Check trees and shrubs for broken branches from winter storms, cut them off cleanly, and apply a tree-wood paint. Rampant vines like honeysuckle should be trimmed back now; rake up accumulated leaves for compost. Remove all other debris that has accumulated over winter because debris breeds insects.

If your container plants have become root bound, repot them and press down heaved soil around edges of boxes and other containers. Wash off soot and dust from all hardy trees and shrubs. This is especially important for evergreens because, unlike deciduous trees, they cannot shed foliage. If dirt is not removed, contamination builds up. If you are economically minded, start summer bulbs indoors for brightening your garden later.

In April continue to plant trees and shrubs as well as container-grown or balled-and-burlapped stock. Prepare soil in boxes or beds so they will be ready for annuals; add humus or leafmold to ensure a nutrious, well-balanced soil. Divide old clumps of summer- and fall-blooming perennials and replant the divisions. Try to have all perennials in the ground by late May. Feed summer-blooming shrubs and lawns with a high-nitrogen fertilizer such as 10-10-5. Depending on the rainfall, start moderate watering. Roof gardens will need more water than backyard gardens, where only newly planted shrubs and trees will need moisture.

May is the month for bedding plants; get seedlings into the ground and put in less tender bulbs like gladiola and cannas. Now is the last chance to get trees and shrubs into the ground, unless they are balled and burlapped or container grown. But even the latter plants will have a better start if they are put into the ground in May.

Increase the watering schedule, especially if you have a roof garden. Keep soil wet so plants have a chance to grow. When warm weather comes, insects become active, so keep a keen eye out for them and catch trouble before it starts. Use the home remedies described in Chapter 10 for pests. If pests are particularly bothersome, select nonpersistent poisons like rotenone and pyrethrum sprays. If mildew becomes a problem, try to water early in the day so the garden is dry by night; if mildew has already started, dust plants with sulfur. May is also the time to introduce natural predators such as lady bugs and praying mantids, which are available from suppliers.

Continue to plant annuals and summer bulbs this month, and don't forget the biennials like foxglove and sweet william, which are available this month at nurseries.

Increase watering at the end of the month, when plants are starting active growth. Keep all foliage washed clean of soot and pollution.

Planting should be over by June, and the garden should be starting its show. Roof gardens need a tremendous amount of water now, and backyard sites, too, need ample moisture to sustain lush growth. Plant summer flowers and pot grown plants like impatiens and caladiums to brighten the scene. Keep feeding plants and pruning shade trees whenever necessary.

Water plants thoroughly in July and August and be ever alert for insects. Lightly prune conifers and feed lawns. Divide perennials and pinch and snip tips of chrysanthemums. Remove dead flower stalks from perennials. Keep dead flowers off of such annuals as marigolds, lantanas, and ageratum.

In September pick dead flowers off annuals, and divide perennials (except late-flowering ones like chrysanthemums and asters). Start to plant some of the smaller bulbs and if rainfall is adequate, water sparingly plants in the backyard garden. Continue regular watering of plants in the roof garden, however, for wind and sun dry out plants.

Now is the best time to put in hardy perennials for summer bloom. They are available in cans or flats and will generally survive the winter without harm.

October and November are the last times to plant. Remove annuals before a killing frost sets in so that it will be easy to plant spring-flowering bulbs. October is the month to plant tulips, hyacinths, and daffodils and also trees and shrubs, unless the ground is already frozen. However, trees like birch and magnolias should be planted in spring. Plant conifers and broad-leaved evergreens now, too. Mulch the evergreens at planting time and keep moist until frost arrives. Do clean-up chores—winter is on the way.

November is the last chance to plant perennials and evergreens. Plant deciduous shrubs and trees as long as the soil is workable. Mulch your garden now, for it is one of the best methods of protecting plants against severe weather.

10. Insects and Disease

The city garden, because it is usually small, should present only small problems. There should never be a great infestation of insects or a plague of disease if plants are tended regularly and growing well. A healthy plant, like a healthy person, is strong and robust, able to resist invaders.

In roof gardens and balcony gardens, where plants are mainly in pots, there are few plant problems, too; here wind and sun, soot and pollution, rather than insects, are likely to be hindrances. So remember that if you do see insects on your plants—in backyard gardens or container plants—do not purchase a barrage of poisons; there are many better ways of eliminating pests.

Is It Insects or Culture?

Not all, or even many, plant problems are caused by insects or disease. Look to care first. Are plants getting enough water and enough light? Or are they getting too much sun? What about wind; is it harming the plant? Determine just what the problem is before you act. For example.

Plants that develop leaves with brown or crisp edges may be getting too much heat and are thus being hindered by fluctuating soil temperatures.

If leaves turn yellow, there may be a lack of acidity in the soil.

If leaves develop brown or silvery streaks, plants are getting too much water.

Whitefly can be a pest in the garden but is easily eliminated with proper controls. (USDA photo)

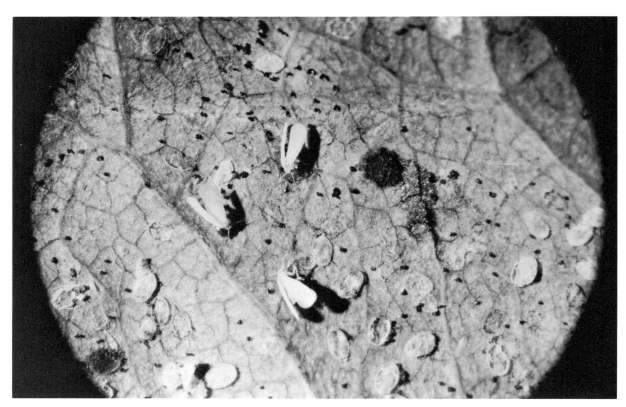

The scourge of many city gardens is mealybug. (USDA photo)

If foliage appears limp and wan, plants are not getting enough water.

Buds suddenly dropping off is caused by fluctuating temperatures.

It may be the natural tendency of a particular plant to develop yellow leaves that drop off. A plant that doesn't do well in one place should be moved to a different location; sometimes this makes all the difference in the world.

If cultural conditions are good and plants still suffer, look for insects. Most common garden pests are recognizable on sight. It is important to know what you are fighting before you do battle. In most cases, even if plants do have insects, poisonous sprays are not necessary. Old-fashioned methods and new biological controls can eliminate most of the culprits.

PREVENTATIVES

One of the best ways to avoid plant problems is to catch them before they start. Observe plants frequently to see if they are growing (new shoots and leaves) or just existing. In the city, soot and dust accumulation on leaves can cause more damage than insects, for they close plant pores and make transpiration impossible. Wash and hose plants frequently. When you hose down plants aim the spray at the bottom of leaves, leaf axils, and hard-to-get-at places where soot and insects can congregate. There are many hose-attachment devices suitable for this; some spray, some create a fine blast of water, and others mist plants. Use the one that best suits your needs.

Even if plants do have insects, try some old-fashioned remedies before resorting to chemical warfare. Soap (laundry soap, not detergent) and water deter aphids; alcohol on a cotton swab makes mealy bugs disappear. Scrape off scale with a stiff toothbrush dipped in soapy water. Picking off insects by hand is good, too, if you are willing to touch the devils.

Other control methods include:

Persistent poisons. Ecologists' main concern is not how poisonous a chemical is, but how persistent and accumulative it is. Researchers have discovered that many years after application, hydrocarbon chemicals such as lindane, aldrin, chlordane, DDT, and dozens of others are still found in living organisms—virtually everywhere on earth. *Avoid any chlorinated hydrocarbons.*

The lacebug may appear handsome, but he is an insidious garden pest. (USDA photo)

Biological control. This is a valid control because it is fighting nature with nature and uses natural predators instead of poisons. Ladybugs, praying mantids, and lacewing bugs are all part of biological control. This method also involves planting onions, marigolds, chrysanthemums, and other plants that naturally repel insects. Birds are also part of the defense. Swallows are excellent insect-eating scavengers, as are purple martins. Another group of beneficial birds are from the flycatcher family, of which the kingbird is a member. His diet consists mainly of insects. Wrens, titmice, and bush tits are other friendly birds that will help to keep your garden insect-free. The Baltimore oriole is still another friend; he consumes caterpillars, pupae, and even adult moths. To have birds in your garden, plant berry bushes such as pyracantha and have water available for the birds. They love water and congregate wherever there is a supply, whether it be from a garden fountain, in a bird bath, or a mist from a water sprinkler.

Systemics. Systemics are poisons such as Di-syston and Meta-systox-R. This is a popular way of killing insects because it is easy and takes little time. Still, *it is highly toxic and cumulative, and per-*

sistent effects have not yet been studied thoroughly, so proceed with caution. Poison comes in granular form (there are also liquids) and should be sprinkled on the ground; the ground should then be watered. Poison is absorbed by plant roots, and all part of the plant become toxic to some insects for a period of four to six weeks. However, systemics only control a few insects—aphids, leaf hoppers, and mealy bugs—and any careful gardener can surely control these without dubious chemcials.

Organic chemicals. These are insect deterents made from plants—chrysanthemums, rotenone, quassia, and others. They are *nonpersistent* and harmless to warm-blooded animals. They are excellent controls, although several applications may be necessary. Organic controls are increasingly being used in combination with other, more lethal poisons. So check the labels on cans and packages carefully to be sure of contents.

As mentioned, ecologists' main concern is not how poisonous a chemical is but how persistent and accumulative it is. The preventatives listed below while still poisonous, are considered nonaccumulative at this time.

THE THOUGHTFUL GARDENER'S GUIDE

INSECTS	WHAT THEY LOOK LIKE	WHAT THEY ATTACK	WHAT THEY DO	CONTROL
Aphids	Green, black, pink, yellow, or red soft-bodied insects	Almost all plants	Stunt plants, deform leaves	Malathion, rotenone
Beetles	Usually brown or black; wingless	Flowers and vegetables	Eat leaves and flowers	Handpick if possible
Caterpillars (includes bagworms, cutworms, cankerworms, tent caterpillars)	Easily recognized	All kinds of plants	Defoliate plants	Rotenone, diazinon, malathion
Grasshoppers	Familiar insect	Plants, trees	Eat leaves	Sevin

Lacebugs	Small bugs with lacy wings	Azaleas; oaks; birches; hawthorns; other plants	Mottle leaves	Malathion
Leaf hoppers	Wedge-shaped insects that hop	Many plants	Turn leaves pale or brown; stunt plants	Malathion
Mealy bugs	White cottony insects	Many plants	Stunt plants so they don't grow	Sevin, diazinon
Mites	Minute sucking insects	Almost all plants	Discolor leaves	Systemics
Nematodes	Microscopic worms	Many plants	Stunt plants so they die back	Sterilize soil
Scale	Tiny, hard, oval insects	Many plants	Yellow leaves or cause them to be lost	Diazinon
Snails, slugs (not insects but common pests)	Easily recognized	Many plants	Eat foliage	Snare-all without Metaldehyde
Springtails	Tiny black jumping bugs	Some plants	Pit leaves	Malathion
Thrips	Tiny winged insects	Few plants	Make leaves silvery	Malathion
Wireworms	Hard, shiny, coiled worms	Flowers, vegetables	Kill seedlings; work underground	Diazinon

SOURCE: Much of the above data is taken from The Thoughtful Gardener's Guide, published in "Cry California," *Journal of California Tomorrow*, Vol. 4, No. 3 (Summer, 1969).

PLANT DISEASES

Bacteria, fungi, and viruses are the cause of several plant diseases, but none are especially severe or likely to attack many plants. Diseases are generally named for their dominant symptoms (blight, canker, leaf spot) or for the organism causing the disease (rust, powdery mildew). These diseases may be prevalent in the rural garden, where there is much more space and more plants, but in the city garden they are rare. However, unfavorable conditions and poor cultural practices open the way for these agents to cause trouble. Excessive

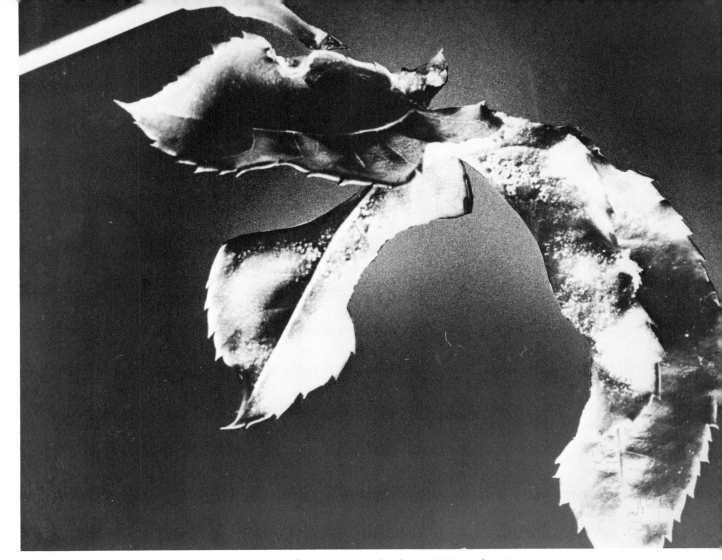

Mildew affects several plants; here it is shown on rose leaflets. (USDA photo)

moisture is particularly important, because it is necessary for the germination of spores of the organism of the disease. Several insects, too, carry diseases from one plant to another.

Some common causes of plant disease are:

Fungi. This is familiar to us because we have seen stale bread, fruit, and mushrooms on which fungi have developed. There are thousands of different kinds of fungi, some of which can cause serous plant damage. Rot, wilt, rust, and powdery mildew are basically caused by specific fungi.

Bacteria. Human diseases are caused by bacteria, and so are several plant ailments. These are microscopic organisms that survive in soil or plant parts and cause blight, rot, galls, or wilting. Bacteria are the causative agent of fire blight and iris rhizome rot.

Viruses. Many of the most serious diseases of ornamental plants are caused by viruses. We are still trying to decipher viruses in humans, and they are as much a mystery when they attack plants.

Here are some plant diseases that may strike plants. As mentioned, although there seem to be many on this list, in reality you will rarely encounter them.

Powdery mildew. White or gray growth usually appearing on the surface of leaves, branches, or fruit. Leaves are powdery, with blotches, and sometimes curled. Plants are often stunted. Control: Hose spray or heavy rain.

Leaf Spot. Can do extensive damage to ornamental plants, resulting in defoliation. Leaves have distinct spots with brownish or white centers and dark edges. Rarely fatal, but affected foliage should be cut off. Control: Spray with zineb or ferbam.

Wilt. Caused by various organisms and can affect mature plants and seedlings. Usually, wilt organisms live in soil. Cut away infected parts. Control: No known chemical control.

Cankers. Lesions on woody stems, with fungi entering through unbroken tissue. Control: Cut away infected parts.

Rose cane infected with canker; cut the cane several inches below the canker and destroy it. (USDA photo)

11. The City Beautiful

In the past few years, there has been an increased interest in home gardens. This interest has spread to the city proper, and rightly so. A green city is not only aesthetically pleasing but also healthful because trees and shrubs and plants of all kinds filter the air and supply the oxygen we breathe. For years Europeans have been aware of what plants can do for an urban area. The boulevards in many of their cities, decorated with handsome trees and gardens, reflect this knowledge and their concern.

Although America started late in the "City Beautiful" program, several cities are now concentrating on gardens for downtown areas. Urban planners realize that plants buffer winds, help absorb noise pollution, and provide cool shade. As a result, in Chicago and San Francisco, St. Louis and New York, tree-lined streets and beautiful parks are finally becoming part of the total picture.

City Plants

Because of the polluted air in many cities, it is difficult to grow plants—but certainly not impossible. Suburban landscaping and planting rules apply to the urban scene, too, but, of course, on a larger scale. The right kinds of trees and shrubs must be used so they will prosper. And prosper they will if they are selected intelligently and planted properly.

In many cities summer heat is intense and hazardous to plants because it is reflected by the concrete surrounding them. Chemical-laden air further thwarts good plant growth. It is thus a challenge indeed to integrate green belts with stone and concrete, but I am happy to say that many city fathers are taking up this challenge and meeting it with success.

In addition to trees and shrubs, seasonal flowering plants are ideal for city display; they supply bright color to cheer people. Today, new city buildings often include several areas for plants: atriums, front gardens, and so forth. A whole new kind of gardening is emerging, and here we shall briefly discuss it.

Highway and freeway officials are also aware of the need to integrate plants with roads. Indeed, the highway departments of some large cities have made a genuine effort to maintain trees and to plant more of them wherever possible. Other cities should follow suit, without further convincing, as nature around us is dwindling quickly.

Lobbies and Offices

As we started to beautify outdoor urban areas, we also convinced builders and architects to include plants in large buildings (mainly in lobbies where the greenery "greets" the public). In New York I am especially impressed to see lush gardens thriving in air conditioning in summer and coping (with fairly good success) with high artificial heat in winter. It is true that the plants may not be growing as well

In the heart of San Francisco is this beautiful garden of the Standard Oil Co. (Photo by Matthew Barr)

More downtown plantings, a mass of colorful beauty. (Photo by Matthew Barr)

as they would in optimum conditions, but at least they are still growing and thus providing necessary beauty.

I don't believe there is really any one secret for growing indoor plants in artificial heat and air conditioning; it is a combination of proper procedures. Although many kinds of plants will not tolerate drafts and fluctuating temperatures, dust and soot, there are an equal number that will. With the controlled heating and adequate humidity that most buildings have, many kinds of plants can be grown. The outstanding ones include palms, bromeliads, some philodendrons, several dracaenas, and *Ficus benjamina* and *F. retusa*. With proper watering and light (artificial light is fine), these plants can grace a lobby or office for years.

PLANNING

Information about how to select plants for indoors is available in several pamphlets and in many garden books. Planning the indoor or outdoor urban garden takes much experience and professional

119

know-how: just which plants to use and how to group them to form visually pleasing green islands is, briefly, what it is all about. (Of course, there is much more to it than that, but further details would require another book!)

A fine example of good outdoor planning is the Standard Oil Building's complex of outdoor plantings in the heart of San Francisco; Chicago and New York, too, have excellent outdoor gardens that add cheer and provide good feeling for passersby.

The landscape architect and the city planner are the guardians of our urban-renewal gardening programs; they perform a service that ensures us of attractive city parks and areas in the future. Let us hope they will continue to try and provide city residents with better living and working areas. Cities have made a start, but it is small compared with what *really* has to be done to bring urban areas back to life, to ensure future generations the benefits of the attractive large cities that we as children enjoyed.

Containers hold abundant bloom in this fine urban city garden, a delight to all passersby. (Photo by Matthew Barr)